FORMAL SPRING

FORMAL SPRING

FRENCH RENAISSANCE POEMS

of

*Charles d'Orléans, Villon
Ronsard, du Bellay
& others*

with translations by
R. N. CURREY

Granger Index Reprint Series

BOOKS FOR LIBRARIES PRESS
FREEPORT, NEW YORK

First published 1950 by
Oxford University Press.
Reprinted 1969 by arrangement

STANDARD BOOK NUMBER:
8369-6054-8

LIBRARY OF CONGRESS CATALOG CARD NUMBER:
76-80372

MANUFACTURED
BY
HALLMARK LITHOGRAPHERS, INC.
IN THE U.S.A.

To my Mother

PREFACE

THE period of these poems, that of the later Middle Ages and the Renaissance, can no longer be looked back upon as a golden age, but it remains exciting. The bright, illuminated colours of the European manuscript softened into light and shade, the stiff figures moved into graceful life, but against a background of famine, squalor, superstition, cruelty, and disease. The towns-people lived over open sewers, crowded to weddings, preachings, and executions, screamed for blood or cried for pity, rang church bells continuously for days, carried on their undersized bodies and sunken faces the marks of horrible diseases, and probably died of the plague. Countrymen scraped infertile soil and tended stunted beasts under conditions of semi-slavery.

It was a period in which France had many connexions with England. The commonalty of language and architecture that began with the Conquest had extended to crusading habits and an Arthurian legend with bases in Brittany as well as Britain; and in this period many poets had some connexion, fortunate or otherwise, with events in England. Villon, the most exclusively French, was aware of the English chiefly as the foreign invaders who had burned Joan of Arc; but Eustache Deschamps recognized in Chaucer, 'great translator' of French writings into English, one of the foremost minds of his age; Christine de Pisan, one of the earliest upholders of the dignity of women, was widely read in England; Charles d'Orléans, captured at Agincourt, spent twenty-five years in England, wrote extensively in English, and married the child-widow of Richard II; Basselin seems to have suffered at the hands of the English 'companies' in the Hundred Years War; Ronsard and du Bellay, learning the sonnet form from the Italian of Petrarch, handed it on to Shakespeare and Sir Philip Sidney; Ronsard, too, in the time of the Scots-French connexion, travelled as a page to Scotland; while the Queen he served, Mary Stuart, represented by one poem in this book, became the ill-fated Queen of Scots who was beheaded in England.

Many of these were court poets, and this had its disadvantages. The literature of the time, ignoring the unspeakable lot of the common people, attributed to the nobility a splendour, style, and sense of chivalry which they rarely possessed. Hysterical, petty, and childish, they gloated over executions, ill-treated their women, quarrelled to the death over questions of precedence, and, so far from living in the splendour suggested by most historical fiction, would often fight on cart-horses with tiny retinues of half-armed footmen, a squire mounted pillion-fashion behind. Ugly little men at 14, they were old and bent at 45: as late as the sixteenth century women were thought to be at their loveliest at 15.

Life in most ways was nasty, brutish, and short—but it was vivid. Against a background of extreme discomfort a seat in the sun for five minutes is exquisite pleasure, a crust and a mouthful of wine paradise. Even for the nobility a rose, a coloured neckerchief, a painted saint on a church wall, glowed and vibrated in the mind like a child's new toy: the beauty of a spring day and the scarcely more lasting loveliness of a woman were felt with an exceptional intensity. The common man could not write, though a scholarly drinking-companion like Villon sometimes expressed his thoughts for him. The nobility made writing the servant of their artificial existence at court, but occasionally a spontaneous emotion was captured in their formal words.

Simplicity grows out of artifice, not artifice out of simplicity. While scholars split hairs in their attempts to equate the teachings of Christ and Aristotle, and inadvertently forged an instrument for accurate scientific deduction, poets struggled to write within a framework of elaborate and rigid forms, and gradually discovered subtler disciplines of poetic expression. Nearly all the vast poetic output of this period was formal exercise, but from time to time a poet with something individual to say would transform rondeau, chanson, or ballade into poetry.

A number of the poems of this period are assembled here opposite English versions. While they form a period collection wide enough—it is hoped—to reflect some of the main characteristics of the age, the primary object in translating them has always been to convey some of the pleasure felt on reading the original poems. At least half of them had been separately done and published before there was any thought of making them into a period volume, and those done since have been attempted for their own sake rather than for period considerations. The period is, nevertheless, a homogeneous one and knowledge of one poet's work helps in the appreciation of another's.

It is a period at once too well known to English readers and not known well enough. Rossetti, Swinburne, and Andrew Lang introduced Villon but failed (inevitably) to reintroduce the ballade and rondel forms in which he and his contemporaries wrote. Mr. Belloc's *Avril* connected the names of Villon and Charles d'Orléans with those of Ronsard and du Bellay, the early with the later Renaissance, and we have had several English studies both of Villon and Ronsard. There have been several complete versions of Villon and partial ones of Ronsard and others, as well as at least one representative anthology of the period—but despite these the pre-Raphaelites with their handful of vivid translations remain the best-known interpreters of the period—and have all too often impressed their style on their successors.

The period made an enormous impression on the pre-Raphaelites, engendering poems as different as 'The Blessed Damozel' and 'The Haystack in the Floods'; but generally their romantic view of the Middle Ages led them into paraphrases as little like the real thing as Ruskin's Gothic. Rossetti, in his famous translation of Villon's 'Ballade des Dames du Temps Jadis'—a translation with that rarest of qualities, a life of its own—has turned 'Dictes moy ou, n'en quel pays' into 'Tell me now in what hidden way is', and the cruel ironical 'Pour son amour ot cest essoyne' into 'From Love he won such dule and teen'; while 'yester-year' overdoes the nostalgia of 'antan'. Villon is direct, unsentimental, almost stark. It is impossible, in translating him, to find few enough, and direct enough, words that will also fit into English verse. In this ballade, too, there is a list of names to be fitted in. The translator is bound to resort to doubtful shifts here and there; 'hidden way is' and 'dule and teen' are only mentioned because Rossetti did not appear to regard them as shifts, but rather seemed proud of them, as men were proud of the battlements on their suburban houses from behind which no archer would ever shoot an arrow! Similarly with Swinburne's rendering of the 'Epitaphe en forme de Ballade', when he spoke of the birds plucking off beards and eyebrows 'for fee', he must have realized that he was adding something for the sake of rhyme, but when he inserted 'perdie' he may have thought it was in keeping with the spirit of the poem. The Victorians often patronised the Middle Ages, speaking what they imagined to be the language of the natives.

It seems necessary to refer at some length to this question of language, as it keeps recurring. A case can be made out for the translation of Ronsard, for instance, into Elizabethan rather than twentieth-century English, as only by this means can his conceits be rendered, but the effect of such essays tends to be quaint at the expense of reality; and, if applied to a poet like Charles d'Orléans, would produce English almost as hard to understand as his French. His own words, for instance: 'Be nyse myn hert as purse is of an ay'[1] hardly convey, without the help of a glossary, a vivid description of a poet's extreme sensitiveness! Henley's vigorous translation of Villon's jargon verse: 'It's up the spout and Charley Wag . . . Booze and the blowens cop the lot' is both quaint and incomprehensible. What does get across seems to have more to do with Bill Sykes than François Villon! Translators who lived before the machine age had a great advantage in that they were describing a form of life not essentially different from their own; but even then most translations were very temporary affairs, parphrasing for the benefit of a single generation only. 'Heraclitus' and 'D'un Vanneur de blé' are English and French exceptions that spring at once to the mind; but it is difficult to appreciate now how Keats could have been quite so transported by Chapman's Homer!

The pseudo-medieval turns of phrase which seemed so fresh to Rossetti have grown dull with frequent use. The large number of stock poetic words which come so easily—'fain', 'amain'; 'aright', 'bedight', &c.—have lost most of their impact. Though they have musical qualities lacking in the speech of to-day, they suggest little more than a vague poetic mood, and it seems that it is only by a plainer approach that the original freshness of these poems can in any degree be caught and communicated.

Preface

The aim, therefore, has been to use contemporary idiomatic English, avoiding slang and other new words which give anachronistic shocks. Archaisms have also been avoided, but Biblical and prayer-book expressions have sometimes been used, as, for example, in translating a prayer. As a rule the form of the original poem has been reproduced as nearly as possible within the English tradition. In the case of one early poem this was modified to avoid intolerable stiffness, but in translating ballades and rondeaux it seems essential to reproduce the repetitions of rhyme and phrase, or else the sense of inevitability is lost. On the other hand both ballade and rondel make extortionate demands on English rhymes, so it has been necessary to choose sometimes between an inexact rhyme and an awkward and unnatural inversion: the former has usually seemed the lesser evil. The aim has always been to give the closest possible rendering of the French consistent with producing a unified version in English; but the fact that these poems have been translated over a period of more than ten years is a source of inconsistency. It is often impossible, after a lapse of time, to get rid of an 'easy' or inaccurate line, except by means which destroy the vitality of the poem as a whole; and attempts at minor revision have usually led to complete retranslation.

Nearly all the poems are complete and translated in full. The few extracts and omissions are clearly shown: in one case only was an omission made on grounds of 'taste' alone, and here the choice was between omission and circumlocution, the former seeming the less prudish alternative. The French text of the passages omitted, with two easily accessible exceptions, is given in a note at the end of the book. There is a bibliography of the main texts and authorities consulted.

We are all, of course, familiar with the argument that there are so many difficulties in verse translation that one had better stick to prose. In the case of a difficult philosophical poem there may be something in this counsel of despair: if there is no hope of smuggling both form and content through the language Customs, then it is better to sacrifice form! But for the carefully shaped verses of the fourteenth, fifteenth, and sixteenth centuries, in which form and content are one, there is no choice for a translator but to attempt the impossible—until a Mr. Arthur Waley does for Charles d'Orléans what he did for *Genji* and invents a new prose (or was it a poetic?) form.

May 1949   R. N. C.

ACKNOWLEDGEMENTS

I SHOULD like to thank the following: Lord David Cecil, C.H., Mr. D. B. Wyndham Lewis, and Mr. Vernon Watkins for valuable encouragement and criticism; Professor A. Ewert for expert criticism at the proof stage; Miss Frances Ambery-Smith, Mr. E. H. Cunningham, and Dr. G. S. Purkis for specialist advice over a period of years, and Mr. H. P. Martin for help with the text also; Mr. Philip Mairet and Mr. Seumas O'Sullivan for taking a personal as well as an editorial interest in so many of these versions. I should like also to record my debt to the late Mr. Edward Thompson for many generous and outspoken comments.

Most of these translations have appeared previously in the periodical press, and some have been broadcast. Acknowledgements are due to the editors of: *The Adelphi, The Dublin Magazine, John O' London's Weekly, The Listener, Modern Languages, The New English Weekly, The Observer, Translation,* and *Time and Tide.* I am obliged to the editor and proprietors of *John O' London's Weekly* for permission to reprint four poems of which they hold copyright. Two of the poems in this collection appeared in my *Tiresias and Other Poems* (O.U.P., 1941) and one in *This Other Planet* (Routledge, 1945); they are reproduced here among poems of their period and with their French originals opposite.

CONTENTS

Contents

Contents

Contents

TEXT AND BIBLIOGRAPHY

*(Where more than one edition of a poet's work is listed, the text used
is that of the first-named, except where otherwise described.)*

P. Tarbé: *Œuvres de Guillaume de Machault*, Rheims et Paris 1849.

Société des Anciens Textes Français, *Œuvres complètes de Eustache Deschamps*, Paris 1878–1903; *Œuvres poétiques de Christine de Pisan*, Paris 1886.

Pierre Champion, *Poésies de Charles d'Orléans*, Paris 1923.

R. Steele, *The English Poems of Charles of Orleans*, London 1941. (O.U.P.)

Auguste Longnon, *Œuvres de François Villon*, Paris 1892, 4th edition revised by Lucien Foulet, Paris 1932.

Louis Thuasne, *Œuvres de François Villon, Édition critique*, Paris 1923.

P. L. Jacob, *Vau de vire d'Olivier Basselin et de Jean Le Houx*, Paris 1858.

Armand Gasté, *Olivier Basselin et le Vau de Vire*, Paris 1887.

M. P. Jannet, *Œuvres complètes de Clément Marot*, Paris 1884.

B. de la Monnoye, *Œuvres complètes de Mellin de Saint-Gelais*, revised by Prosper Blanchemain, Paris 1873.

P. Laumonier, *Œuvres complètes de P. de Ronsard* (1584 text), Paris 1914–19.

Hugues de Vaganay, *Œuvres complètes de Ronsard, texte de 1578*, Paris 1923–4.

Henri Chamard, *Œuvres poétiques de Joachim du Bellay, Édition critique*, Paris 1908–31.

Charles Boy, *Œuvres de Louise Labé*, Paris 1887.

Gauthier-Ferrières, *Anthologie des XVe et XVIe siècles* (for lines attributed to Marie Stuart), Paris 1913.

J. Sharman, *The Poems of Mary Queen of Scots*, London 1873.

St. John Lucas, *The Oxford Book of French Verse*, Oxford 1926.

Pierre Champion, *Histoire poétique du quinzième siècle*, Paris 1923.

J. Huizinga, *The Waning of the Middle Ages*, London 1924. (Edward Arnold.)

Hilaire Belloc, *Avril, Essays on the Poetry of the French Renaissance*, London 1904. (Duckworth.)

Pierre Champion, *François Villon, sa vie et son temps*, Paris 1913.

D. B. Wyndham Lewis, *François Villon—A Documented Survey*, London 1928. (Peter Davies.)

Italo Siciliano, *François Villon et les thèmes poétiques du moyen âge*, Paris 1934.

Edward F. Chaney, *François Villon and his Environment*, Oxford 1946. (Blackwell.)

P. Laumonier, *Ronsard*, Paris 1923.

D. B. Wyndham Lewis, *Ronsard*, London 1944. (Sheed and Ward.)

Shorter studies include R. L. Stevenson's essays on Charles d'Orléans and Villon in *Familiar Studies of Men and Books*, and Walter Pater's essay on Du Bellay in *The Renaissance*. Translations of Villon in full include those of John Payne, H. de Vere Stacpoole, John Heron Lepper, Lewis Wharton, Geoffrey Atkinson, H. B. McCaskie, and Edward Chaney. The other poets in this book have been more scantily translated: Humbert Wolfe's versions of Ronsard's *Sonnets pour Hélène* are notable.

FORMAL SPRING

GUILLAUME DE MACHAULT

GUILLAUME DE MACHAULT (c. 1300–1377)
had great influence on the poetic forms of this period. In
80,000 lines of elaborate verse-forms and intricate rhyme-
schemes he said very little of importance, but it was within
this formal framework that French poetry developed and
such individual masterpieces as Villon's greatest ballades
were written. Had he managed to infuse any genuine feeling
into his exquisitely fashioned forms he might have been as
well known as Petrarch—like whom, incidentally, he spun
out endless verses to a lady who married somebody else.
Secretary to the King of Bohemia; canon of Rheims; he
was also a musician: he set some of his own work to music
and composed a mass for Charles V's coronation.

RONDEAU

BLANCHE com lys, plus que rose vermeille,
Resplendissant com rubis d'oriant,
En remirant vo biauté non pareille
Blanche com lys, plus que rose vermeille,
Suy si ravis, que mes cuers toudis veille
Afin que serve, à loy de fin amant,
Blanche com lys, plus que rose vermeille,
Resplendissant com rubis d'oriant.

RONDEAU

WHITE as a lily, redder than a rose,
Bright as a ruby from the Orient,
I stare and stare while your rare beauty glows
White as a lily, redder than a rose;
So overcome, that I keep watch with those
Who serve for ever by love's precedent:
White as a lily, redder than a rose;
Bright as a ruby from the Orient.

EUSTACHE DESCHAMPS

EUSTACHE DESCHAMPS (*c.* 1340–*c.* 1410) *held various feudal offices at the courts of Charles V and VI, and his voluminous writings give many details of the life of his time. The girl in his 'Virelay' belongs against a background of castles like those painted by the Limburg brothers for the Duke of Berry's 'Book of Hours', which was begun in 1409. He did much to establish the rondel and ballade forms, giving them a more realistic content than most poets who came before and many who came after. His ballade to Chaucer gives an interesting commentary on a man whose outstanding claim to fame in the eyes of French contemporaries was that he had translated the* Roman de la Rose *for the barbaric inhabitants of England.*

. . . Sowed flowers and planted out the rose-tree
   there,
For you will serve those ignorant of our speech,
O great translator, noble Geoffrey Chaucer.[2]

VIRELAY

Sui je, sui je, sui je belle?

Il me semble, a mon avis,
Que j'ay beau front et doulz viz
Et la bouche vermeillette;
Dittes moy se je suis belle.

J'ay vers yeulx, petits sourcis,
Le chief blont, le nez traitis,
Ront menton, blanche gorgette;
Sui je, sui je, sui je belle?

J'ay dur sain et hault assis,
Lons bras, gresles doys aussis,
Et par le faulz sui greslette;
Dittes moy se je suis belle.

J'ay bonnes rains, ce m'est vis,
Bon dos, bon cul de Paris,
Cuisses et gambes bien faictes;
Sui je, sui je, sui je belle?

J'ay piez rondès et petiz,
Bien chaussans, et biaux habits,
Je suis gaye et joliette;
Dittes moy se je suis belle.

VIRELAY

AM I, am I beautiful?

It seems to me that I possess
A good brow and a pretty face
And a rosy mouth as well:
Tell me, am I beautiful?

Shining eyes with dainty brows,
Blond hair and a well-shaped nose,
Rounded cheeks, throat white and small:
Do these make me beautiful?

High firm breasts, as they ought to be,
Fingers and hands made slenderly,
And such a slender figure: Tell
Me please, if I am beautiful.

Good back, good waist—would you agree?—
Trim bottom, and such pleasantly
Rounded legs and thighs, and—well,
Would you call me beautiful?

Small plump feet in stylish shoes,
And plenty of expensive clothes—
And always gay and cheerful:
Tell me, am I beautiful?

J'ay mantiaux fourrez de gris,
J'ay chapiaux, j'ay biaux proffis
Et d'argent mainte espinglette;
Sui je, sui je, sui je belle?

J'ay draps de soye et tabis,
J'ay draps d'or et blans et bis,
J'ay mainte bonne chosette;
Dittes moy se je sui belle.

Que .xv. ans n'ay, je vous dis;
Moult est mes tresors jolys,
S'en garderay la clavette;
Sui je, sui je, sui je belle?

Bien devra estre hardis
Cilz qui sera mes amis,
Qui ara tel damoiselle;
Dittes moy se je sui belle.

Et par Dieu je li plevis
Que tresloyal, se je vis,
Li seray, si ne chancelle;
Sui je, sui je, sui je belle?

Se courtois est et gentilz,
Vaillans après, bien apris,
Il gaignera sa querelle;
Dittes moy se je sui belle.

Virelay

Coats furred tastefully with grey,
Lots of hats and trimmings gay,
With many a silver pin as well;
Do you think I'm beautiful?

Silk and taffeta draperies
In whites and golds and brownish-greys—
Too many pretty things to tell:
Am I really beautiful?

Only just fifteen, and see
What a treasure belongs to me—
And so I keep the key! . . . Oh tell,
Tell me, am I beautiful?

Any man who hopes to be
The lover of a girl like me
Must be brave and masterful:
Am I, am I beautiful?

But I swear that I will be
True while he unwaveringly
Shows me he is dutiful:
Do you think I'm beautiful?

If he has poise and courtesy,
Courage and breeding too, then he
Shall win what he desires in full:
Am I really beautiful?

C'est uns mondains paradiz
Que d'avoir dame toudiz
Ainsi fresche, ainsi nouvelle;
Sui je, sui je, sui je belle?

Entre vous acouardiz,
Pensez a ce que je diz;
Cy fine ma chansonnette;
Sui je, sui je, sui je belle?

Virelay

Earthly paradise to win
And keep for ever such a one,
So fresh, so new. . . . And now please tell,
Tell me if I'm beautiful?

All you timid ones, agree;
Consider what you've heard from me;
For here ends my canticle:
Am I, am I beautiful?

CHRISTINE DE PISAN

CHRISTINE DE PISAN (*c.* 1363–*c.* 1430), '*bourgeois poetess at a bourgeois court*'—*that of Charles V*—*wrote poems to make money to bring up her family when left a widow at 25. Daughter of Thomas de Pisan, the King's astrologer, she was born in Italy, but came to France as a child. She wrote in defence of women, in particular against the description of feminine character given in the later part of the* Roman de la Rose, *and used Joan of Arc as an example of feminine excellence in her* Dittie de Jeanne d'Arc.

RONDEL

SE souvent vais au moustier,
C'est tout pour veoir la belle
Fresche com rose nouvelle.

D'en parler n'est nul mestier,
Pour quoy fait on tel nouvelle
Se souvent vais au moustier?

Il n'est voye ne sentier
Ou je voise que pour elle;
Folz est qui fol m'en appelle
Se souvent vais au moustier.

RONDEL

IF I'm at church these days
It's just to see her there,
Fresh as new roses are.

Why gossip, then, and raise
Interest in the affair,
If I'm at church these days?

Whatever paths or ways
I follow lead to her;
Fool, to say fool, and stare
If I'm at church these days.

CHARLES D'ORLÉANS

CHARLES D'ORLÉANS (1394–1465), *head of the House of Orléans, nephew of one French King and father of another, is the archetype of the court poet of the waning Middle Ages; his life has the colours of an illuminated manuscript—in all its contemporary splendour. Eldest son of Louis I of Orléans, who was assassinated in 1407 by men in the pay of the Duke of Burgundy, the years in which he grew up were occupied with the consequent vendetta.*

His rank made him, at just under 21, titular commander of the 'flower of European chivalry' overwhelmed by the English bowmen at Agincourt, and he was chief among those captured and held to ransom after the battle. It was twenty-five years before he was able to return to his native country—during which time Joan of Arc saved his ducal city of Orléans, and the affairs of his house were looked after by the Bastard, Dunois, his much abler half-brother. On returning to France he lived in colourful, disillusioned retirement at Blois, surrounded by artists, jongleurs, and poets—among whom for a short time was Villon—and wrote a large number of chansons, rondeaux, and ballades. His poems lack depth, and most are frankly escapist, but every now and then, as in the 'Ballade for Peace' and some of the spring rondeaux, sincere feeling shines through the formal outline.

He had a further connexion with England, in that his first marriage, in 1406, was to the child-widow of the deposed Richard II. During his captivity, too, he wrote nearly 7,000 lines of poetry in English, about half of them with analogues among his French poems. Holinshed says he was more at home speaking English than French at the time of his return. There is now no reasonable doubt that the English poems were his; and it also seems likely that many of them were written in the household of Chaucer's granddaughter, the Countess of Suffolk.

BALLADE LXXVI[3]

PRIÉS pour paix, doulce Vierge Marie,
Royne des cieulx, et du monde maistresse,
Faictes prier, par vostre courtoisie,
Saints et saintes, et prenés vostre adresse
Vers vostre filz, requerant sa haultesse
Qu'il lui plaise son peuple regarder,
Que de son sang a voulu racheter,
En deboutant guerre qui tout desvoye;
De prieres ne vous vueilliez lasser:
Priez pour paix, le vray tresor de joye!

Priez, prelas et gens de sainte vie,
Religieux ne dormez en peresse,
Priez, maistres et tous suivans clergie,
Car par guerre fault que l'estude cesse;
Moustiers destruis sont sans qu'on les redresse,
Le service de Dieu vous fault laissier.
Quant ne povez en repos demourer,
Priez si fort que briefment Dieu vous oye;
L'Eglise voult a ce vous ordonner:
Priez pour paix, le vray tresor de joye!

Priez, princes qui avez seigneurie,
Roys, ducs, contes, barons plains de noblesse,
Gentilz hommes avec chevalerie,
Car meschans gens surmontent gentillesse;
En leurs mains ont toute vostre richesse,

BALLADE FOR PEACE

O PRAY for our peace, sweet Virgin Mary,
Queen of the heavens and the earth's mistress,
And bid the saints pray too, for courtesy,
Women as well as men; in gentleness
Approach your Son, in his exaltedness,
To take thought for his people in this day,
Whose ransom he once gave his life to pay,
By ending war that must all things destroy;
And do not tire of praying when you pray—
But pray for peace, the very heart of joy.

Pray prelates, and all men of sanctity,
Friars and monks, who sleep in idleness,
And scholars, and all learned company,
For war must always mean that studies cease,
And churches are destroyed that none redress,
And services neglected in that day;
Now that your peace and quiet have gone their way
Pray so that God hear soon, not shy or coy,
But as the Church has ordered you to pray,
And pray for peace, the very heart of joy.

Pray kings, and princes, and nobility,
Barons, and counts, and men of courtliness,
And gentle knights brought up in chivalry,
For evil men are killing gentleness;
Your wealth is spoil for their wickedness;

Debatz les font en hault estat monter,
Vous le povez chascun jour veoir au cler,
Et sont riches de voz biens et monnoye
Dont vous deussiez le peuple suporter:
Priez pour paix, le vray tresor de joye!

Priez, peuple qui souffrez tirannie,
Car voz seigneurs sont en telle foiblesse
Qu'ilz ne peuent vous garder, par maistrie,
Ne vous aidier en vostre grant destresse;
Loyaulx marchans, la selle si vous blesse
Fort sur le dox; chascun vous vient presser
Et ne povez marchandise mener,
Car vous n'avez seur passage ne voye,
Et maint peril vous couvient il passer:
Priez pour paix, le vray tresor de joye!

. . . .

Dieu tout puissant nous vueille conforter!
Toutes choses en terre, ciel et mer,
Priez vers lui que brief en tout pourvoye;
En lui seul est de tous maulx amender:
Priez pour paix, le vray tresor de joye!

Ballade for Peace

By violence and strife they force their way
To rank and power—you see it every day!—
Using the money you could well employ
To be your people's comfort and their stay;
So pray for peace, the very heart of joy.

Pray, people who are suffering tyranny;
The lords you serve are now so powerless
They can no longer use their mastery
To guard and save you in your great distress;
And loyal merchants, whom all men oppress,
The yoke is heavy on your backs to-day
When there is no safe-conduct and no way
Is free from gravest danger and annoy
To men who carry merchandise.   O pray—
And pray for peace, the very heart of joy.

God in his power comfort us to-day;
Let heaven and earth and sea unite to pray
That He may soon provide all we enjoy—
For He alone can turn our ills away:
O pray for peace, the very heart of joy!

RONDEL XXXI

L E temps a laissié son manteau
De vent, de froidure et de pluye,
Et s'est vestu de brouderie,
De soleil luyant, cler et beau.

Il n'y a beste, ne oyseau,
Qu'en son jargon ne chante ou crie:
Le temps (a laissié son manteau.)

Riviere, fontaine et ruisseau
Portent, en livree jolie,
Gouttes d'argent d'orfaverie,
Chascun s'abille de nouveau:
Le temps (a laissié son manteau.)

RONDEL

THE year has put his cloak away
His cloak of cold, and wind, and rain,
To wear the embroidery again
Of radiant sunlight, clear and gay.

No bird or beast but joins to-day
His song or jargon in this strain:
The year has put his cloak away,
His cloak of cold, and wind, and rain.

Rivulet, stream, and spring to-day
Wear as splendid livery
Spangles of silver filigree,
All of them in new clothes to-day;
The year has put his cloak away.

RONDEL XXX

LES fourriers d'Esté sont venus
Pour appareillier son logis,
Et ont fait tendre ses tappis,
De fleurs et verdure tissus.

En estandant tappis velus,
De vert herbe par le païs,
Les fourriers (d'Esté sont venus.)

Cueurs d'ennuy pieça morfondus,
Dieu mercy, sont sains et jolis;
Alez vous ent, prenez païs,
Yver, vous ne demourrés plus;
Les fourriers (d'Esté sont venus!)

RONDEL

SUMMER has sent his stewards on
To put his house in readiness,
To hang up woven tapestries
Of flowers and foliage, and put down

Rough carpets of green grass to run
Across the country's emptiness;
Summer has sent his stewards on
To put his house in readiness.

Those who've been gloomy and cast down,
Thank God, have health and happiness.
Be off, then, to some other place;
Winter, you *shall not* linger on!
Summer has sent his stewards on.

RONDEL XXXIV

E N regardant ces belles fleurs
Que le temps nouveau d'Amours prie,
Chascune d'elles s'ajolie
Et farde de plaisans couleurs.

Tant enbasmees sont de odeurs
Qu'il n'est cueur qui ne rajeunie,
En regardant (ces belles fleurs.)

Lez oyseaus deviennent danseurs
Dessuz mainte branche flourie,
Et font joyeuse chanterie,
De contres, deschans et teneurs,
En regardant (ces belles fleurs.)

RONDEL

As we look at these gay flowers
Love's new season has on show,
Let each put on new beauty now,
And paint in her most pleasing colours;

They are so drenched in freshest odours
That every heart feels younger now,
As we look at these gay flowers. . . .

While the birds, becoming dancers
Over many a flowering bough,
Make such a joyful singing now
With their airs, descants, and counters:
As we look at these gay flowers.

RONDEL XXXIX

LE premier jour du mois de may,
De tanné et de vert perdu,
Las! j'ay trouvé mon cuer vestu,
Dieu scet en quel piteux array!

Tantost demandé je lui ay
Dont estoit cest abit venu,
Le premier jour (du mois de may.)

Il m'a respondu: 'Bien le sçay,
Mais par moy ne sera congneu;
Desplaisance m'en a pourveu,
Sa livree je porteray,
Le premier jour (du mois de may.')

RONDEL

THE first day of the month of May
Of tawny, winter-soiled green,
And my poor heart, God knows, is seen
In very shabby clothes to-day.

Tell me, I asked my heart to-day,
What does this style of dressing mean,
The first day of the month of May?

My heart replied, I shall not say,
But know too well why I have been
Engaged to sadness and to spleen;
I wear their livery, take their pay,
This first day of the month of May.

BALLADE XCVII

UNG jour a mon cuer devisoye,
Qui en secret a moy parloit,
Et en parlant lui demendoye
Se point d'espargne fait avoit
D'aucuns biens, quant Amours servoit?
Il me dit que tresvoulentiers
La verité m'en compteroit,
Mais qu'eust visité ses papiers.

Quant ce m'eust dit, il print sa voye
Et d'avecques moy se partoit;
Aprés entrer je le veoye
En ung comptouer qu'il avoit;
La deça et dela queroit,
En cherchant plusieurs vieulx cayers,
Car le vray monstrer me vouloit,
Mais qu'eust visité ses papiers.

Ainsi, par un temps l'atendoye.
Tantost devers moy retournoit
Et me monstra, dont j'eux grant joye,
Ung livre qu'en sa main tenoit,
Ouquel dedens escript portoit
Ses faiz, au long et bien entiers,
Desquelz informer me feroit,
Mais qu'eust visité ses papiers.

BALLADE

ONE day I asked my heart,
In confidence, if he
Had put by any part
Out of our property
When serving Love? Freely
He promised me a true
Account as soon as he
Had looked his papers through.

He promised this, my heart,
And took his leave of me;
And soon I saw him start
To rummage busily
Among the note-books he
Keeps in his desk. I knew
He'd speak immediately
He'd looked his papers through.

I waited, and my heart,
Returning presently,
Showed me the books he'd brought,
And I was glad to see
That he had carefully
Entered the facts—so now
I'd know as soon as he
Had looked his papers through.

Lors demenday se g'y liroye,
Ou se mieulx lire lui plaisoit?
Il dit que trop peine prendroye.
Pourtant a lire commançoit;
Et puis getoit et assommoit
Le conte des biens et dangiers
Tout a ung; vy que revendroye,
Mais qu'eust visité ses papiers.

Lors dy: 'Jamais je ne cuidoye,
Ne nul autre ne le croiroit,
Qu'en amer, ou chascun s'employe,
De prouffit n'eust plus grant exploit;
Amours ainsi les gens deçoit,
Plus ne m'aura en telz santiers.
Mon cuer bien efacier pourroit,
Mais qu'eust visité ses papiers.'

Amours savoir ne me devroit
Mal gré, se blasme ses mestiers;
Il verroit mon gaing bien estroit,
Mais qu'eust visité ses papiers.

Ballade

I asked if I should start
On them myself, but he
Politely begged me not
To trouble; expertly
Began to add for me
Profits and losses too—
Bade me come back when he
Had looked his papers through.

I said: 'I never thought,
And no-one would, to see
Love, in which all take part,
Show such small gains. Thus he
Cheats us, but won't cheat me
Again! My heart might do
Some rubbing out—when he
Has looked his papers through!'

Love should not censure me
For blaming him—he'll know
How small my gains . . . when he
Has looked his papers through!

CHANSON LXXIV

GARDEZ le trait de la fenestre,
Amans, qui par ruez passez,
Car plus tost en serez blessez
Que de trait d'arc ou d'arbalestre.

N'alez a destre ne a senestre
Regardant, mais les yeulx bessez:
Gardez (le trait de la fenestre,)
(Amans, qui par ruez passez.)

Se n'avez medicin, bon maistre,
Si tost que vous serez navrez
A Dieu soyez recommandez;
Mors vous tiens, demandez le prestre:
Gardez (le trait de la fenestre!)

SONG

LOVERS, avoid the shafts that fly
Out of the windows of a street;
Arrows and bolts cannot compete
In swiftness and in certainty;

Turn right nor left, but keep your eye
Upon the ground before your feet;
Lovers, avoid the shafts that fly
Out of the windows of a street.

Unless there is a doctor by,
A good one, right there in the street,
Send for a priest at once, entreat
God's mercy and prepare to die:
Lovers, avoid the shafts that fly . . .

RONDEL XIX[4]

MAISTRE Estienne Le Gout, nominatif,
Nouvellement, par maniere optative,
Si a voulu faire copulative;
Mais failli a en son cas genitif.

Il avoit mis .vj. ducatz en datif,
Pour mielx avoir s'amie vocative,
Maistre Estienne (Le Gout, nominatif.)

Quant rencontré a un acusatif
Qui sa robe lui a fait ablative;
De fenestre assez superlative
A fait un sault portant coups en passif,
Maistre Estienne (Le Gout, nominatif.)

RONDEL

STEPHEN LE GOUT, in the nominative,
Quite recently tried in the optative
Mood to proceed to the copulative,
But failed when it came to the genitive.

Six ducats he placed in the dative
To bring him his love in the vocative—
Stephen Le Gout, in the nominative.

He came up against an accusative
Who made of his robe a mere ablative;
From a window whose height was superlative
He jumped, taking blows in the passive:
Stephen Le Gout, in the nominative.

RONDEL CCCXXXIII

YVER, vous n'estes qu'un villain,
Esté est plaisant et gentil,
En tesmoing de May et d'Avril
Qui l'acompaignent soir et main.

Esté revest champs, bois et fleurs,
De sa livree de verdure
Et de maintes autres couleurs,
Par l'ordonnance de Nature.

Mais vous, Yver, trop estes plain
De nege, vent, pluye et grezil;
On vous deust banir en essil.
Sans point flater, je parle plain,
Yver, (vous n'estes qu'un villain!)

RONDEL

WINTER, you're nothing but a lout.
Summer is polite and gentle;
Only look how May and April
Accompany him day in, day out.

See how fields and woods and flowers
Wear his livery of verdure
And of many other colours
According to the rule of Nature;

But, Winter, you are all filled out
With snow and sleet and wind and drizzle;
It's time we sent you into exile;
I never flatter, but speak out;
Winter, you're nothing but a lout.

FRANÇOIS VILLON

FRANÇOIS VILLON (1431–?). *One of the very few poets of this period who were not court-poets; popular and realistic in an age of well-bred poetry of escape. His real name seems to have been Montcorbier, but he took the name of a chaplain of Saint Benoît who brought him up. He studied at Paris, where he was a member of the University, and took his M.A. degree in 1452, but led a disorderly life and in 1455 killed a priest in a brawl. He left Paris, and wandered in different parts of France, usually in criminal company. For a time he was one of the literary company at Charles d'Orléans's court at Blois, but this did not last; the 'Ballade Villon' which he wrote there mentions a pension which for some reason or other had been taken away from him. Later we hear of him being freed from the prison of the Bishop of Orléans, a lucky chance, since he happened to be there when the doors were opened in celebration of the reigning monarch! In 1462 he was condemned to death at the Châtelet for a second murder, and it was then that he wrote his 'Epitaph in Ballade Form', a poignant personal complaint that was something new in European literature. In his two 'Testaments' we move in the cruel medieval Paris, whose streets were infested on winter nights by the 'wolves that live on wind'; among bawds, prostitutes, housebreakers, and pickpockets; yet, to an extent that makes him outstanding, not only in his own but in every age, he found all experience a subject for poetry. The 'Ballade of the Women of the Past' has a lyrical quality that defies translation. Villon wrote ballades, a few rondeaux, and eight-lined verses with a regular rhyme-scheme: verse of an ordered, formal pattern that perhaps satisfied him as a complement to his disorderly life.*

L'EPITAPHE VILLON[5]

FRERES humains qui après nous vivez,
N'ayez les cuers contre nous endurcis,
Car, se pitié de nous povres avez,
Dieu en aura plus tost de vous mercis,
Vous nous voiez cy attachez cinq, six:
Quant de la chair, que trop avons nourrie,
Elle est pieça devorée et pourrie,
Et nous, les os, devenons cendre et pouldre.
De nostre mal personne ne s'en rie;
Mais priez Dieu que tous nous vueille absouldre!

Se freres vous clamons, pas n'en devez
Avoir desdaign, quoy que fusmes occis
Par justice. Toutesfois, vous sçavez
Que tous hommes n'ont pas bon sens rassis;
Excusez nous, puis que sommes transsis,
Envers le fils de la Vierge Marie,
Que sa grace ne soit pour nous tarie,
Nous preservant de l'infernale fouldre.
Nous sommes mors, ame ne nous harie;
Mais priez Dieu que tous nous vueille absouldre!

La pluye nous a debuez et lavez,
Et le soleil dessechiez et noircis;
Pies, corbeaulx, nous ont les yeux cavez,
Et arrachié la barbe et les sourcis.

VILLON'S
EPITAPH IN BALLADE FORM
(Written while waiting with his companions to be hanged)

O BROTHER men, who live on after us,
You should not in your hearts be too severe,
For if you pity wretches such as us
Then God shall pity you the readier;
Some five or six of us are strung up here,
The flesh we nourished all too lavishly
Has rotted and been devoured utterly,
While we, the bones, in dust and ashes fall;
Let no man laugh at our extremity
But pray to God that He forgive us all.

Why should you think it so presumptuous
Of those who suffered death by law to dare
To call you brothers still; not all of us,
As you know well, have common sense to spare:
Now that we're dead, forgive, and offer prayer
Before the Virgin Mary's Son, that He
Spare mercy even for us, and graciously
Preserve us from Hell's lightnings when they fall.
We're dead. Let none torment our misery,
But pray to God that He forgive us all.

The rain has thoroughly washed and whitened us
And the sun dried and blackened us up here;
The crows and magpies have gouged out our eyes,
Ripped out our beards and plucked our eyebrows bare;

47

Jamais nul temps nous ne sommes assis;
Puis ça, puis la, comme le vent varie,
A son plaisir sans cesser nous charie,
Plus becquetez d'oiseaulx que dez a couldre.
Ne soiez donc de nostre confrairie;
Mais priez Dieu que tous nous veuille absouldre!

Prince Jhesus, qui sur tous a maistrie,
Garde qu'Enfer n'ait de nous seigneurie:
A luy n'ayons que faire ne que souldre.
Hommes, icy n'a point de mocquerie;
Mais priez Dieu que tous nous veuille absouldre!

Epitaph in Ballade Form

At no time may we rest, but always veer
This way and that way, turning helplessly,
At the wind's pleasure carried endlessly,
So pecked we're pitted like thimbles; do not fall
As we did into this fraternity,
But pray to God that He forgive us all.

Prince Jesus, having all authority,
Let us not fall beneath Hell's sovereignty;
Grant that we have no dealings there at all.
Men, there is no excuse for mockery,
But pray to God that He forgive us all.

LE TESTAMENT XXXVIII–XLI
ET BALLADE

SI ne suis, bien le considere,
Filz d'ange portant dyademe
D'estoille ne d'autre sidere.
Mon pere est mort, Dieu en ait l'ame!
Quant est du corps, il gist soubz lame.
J'entens que ma mere mourra,
El le scet bien, la povre femme,
Et le filz pas ne demourra.

Je congnois que povres et riches,
Sages et folz, prestres et laiz,
Nobles, villains, larges et chiches,
Petiz et grans, et beaulx et laiz,
Dames a rebrassez colletz,
De quelconque condicion,
Portans atours et bourreletz,
Mort saisit sans excepcion.

Et meure Paris ou Helaine,
Quiconques meurt, meurt a douleur
Telle qu'il pert vent et alaine;
Son fiel se creve sur son cuer,
Puis sue, Dieu scet quelle sueur!
Et n'est qui de ses maux l'alege:
Car enfant n'a, frere ne seur,
Qui lors voulsist estre son plege.

LINES ON DEATH, AND BALLADE

I'M sure I make no claim to be
An angel's son, in diadem
Of single stars or galaxy;
My father's dead, God pity him!
His body lies beneath his tomb,
And my poor mother must prepare,
As well she knows, to follow him,
And soon her son must follow her.

I only know that poor and rich,
Wise men and foolish, generous, mean,
Great men and humble, lay and church,
Nobles and peasants, handsome, plain,
Ladies with turned-back collars, none,
Whatever her degree or station,
What tire or common headdress on,
None but must die, without exception.

Though Paris die, and Helen too,
Whoever dies, must die in pain,
Feeling his power of breathing go;
Over his heart his gall bursts then;
God, how the cold sweats from him drain;
And none relieves his agony,
Child, brother, sister, there's no one
Who at that time his pledge would be.

La mort le fait fremir, pallir,
Le nez courber, les vaines tendre,
Le col enfler, la chair mollir,
Joinctes et nerfs croistre et estendre.
Corps femenin, qui tant es tendre,
Poly, souef, si precieux,
Te fauldra il ces maux attendre?
Oy, ou tout vif aller es cieulx.

BALLADE

(DES DAMES DU TEMPS JADIS)

DICTES moy ou, n'en quel pays,
Est Flora la belle Rommaine,
Archipiades, ne Thaïs,
Qui fut sa cousine germaine,
Echo parlant quant bruyt on maine
Dessus riviere ou sus estan,
Qui beaulté ot trop plus qu'humaine.
Mais ou sont les neiges d'antan?

Ou est la tres sage Helloïs,
Pour qui chastré fut et puis moyne
Pierre Esbaillart a Saint Denis?
Pour son amour ot ceste essoyne.
Semblablement, ou est la royne
Qui commanda que Buridan
Fust geté en ung sac en Saine?
Mais ou sont les neiges d'antan?

Death makes him shudder and turn white,
His flesh grow soft, his neck distend,
His nose grow hooked, his veins stretch tight,
His joints and sinews swell, extend.
O, woman's body, so smooth-skinned,
Tender, soft, precious, must *you* even
Be brought by fate to such an end?
Yes, or else go alive to heaven.

BALLADE

(OF THE WOMEN OF THE PAST)

O TELL me where and to what land
Has lovely Roman Flora gone,
Where is Archipiada, and
Thaïs, who was her kinswoman,
Echo, whose voice answers one
Over rivers and over meres—
Whose beauty more than human shone:
But where are the snows of other years?

Where learnèd Heloïse, ordained
To bring poor Peter Abelard down
To be made monk, but first unmanned—
This was the judgement his love won!—
And, tell me, where has that Queen gone
Who had that Buridan of hers
Thrown in a sack into the Seine:
But where are the snows of other years?

La royne Blanche comme lis
Qui chantoit a voix de seraine,
Berte au grant pié, Bietris, Alis,
Haremburgis qui tint le Maine,
Et Jehanne la bonne Lorraine
Qu'Englois brulerent a Rouan;
Ou sont ilz, ou, Vierge souvraine?
Mais ou sont les neiges d'antan?

Prince, n'enquerez de sepmaine
Ou elles sont, ne de cest an,
Qu'a ce reffrain ne vous remaine:
Mais ou sont les neiges d'antan?

And Queen Blanche, of the lily hand
And siren's voice, where is she gone?
Big-footed Bertha, Beatrice, and
Alice, Arembour, who alone
Ruled all the Maine, and Lorraine Joan,
Burned at Rouen in English fires:
O Virgin Queen, where are they gone;
But where are the snows of other years?

Prince, do not ask where they are gone
This week, this year, for all your prayers
Can win back one refrain alone:
But where are the snows of other years?

BALLADE[6]

Je meurs de seuf auprès de la fontaine,
Chault comme feu, et tremble dent a dent;
En mon païs, suis en terre loingtaine;
Lez ung brasier frissonne tout ardent;
Nu comme ung ver, vestu en president,
Je ris en pleurs et attens sans espoir;
Confort reprens en triste desespoir;
Je m'esjouÿs, et n'ay plaisir aucun;
Puissant je suis sans force et sans povoir,
Bien recueully, debouté de chascun.

Rien ne m'est seur que la chose incertaine;
Obscur, fors ce qui est tout evident;
Doubte ne fais, fors en chose certaine;
Science tiens a soudain accident;
Je gaigne tout et demeure perdent;
Au point du jour dis: 'Dieu vous doint bon soir!'
Gisant envers, j'ay grant paour de cheoir;
J'ay bien de quoy et si n'en ay pas ung;
Eschoitte attens et d'omme ne suis hoir,
Bien recueully, debouté de chascun.

De riens n'ay soing, si mectz toute ma paine
D'acquerir biens et n'y suis pretendent;
Qui mieulx me dit, c'est cil qui plus m'attaine,
Et qui plus vray, lors plus me va bourdent;
Mon amy est, qui me fait entendent

BALLADE

I DIE of thirst beside the fountain's brim,
As hot as fire, with my teeth chattering,
In my own land a stranger, a pilgrim;
Beside a brazier I stand shivering,
Bare as a worm, in rich appareling;
I laugh in tears, while waiting hopeless here
And taking comfort of my sad despair;
Rejoicing, although pleasure I have none,
Powerful, with nothing that I can or dare—
Welcomed by all, and he whom all men shun.

Nothing is sure to me except a whim,
Obscure, except the clear and obvious thing,
Only in certainties my faith is dim,
And knowledge has an adventitious ring;
I am the loser, gaining everything;
At dawn I bid good evening, and I fear,
While lying prone, lest I should fall from there;
I'm rich, and have no coin beneath the sun,
Expect a legacy, though no man's heir,
Welcomed by all, and he whom all men shun.

I care for nothing; taking care to trim
My course for profit, claim no single thing;
The man who flatters most, I'm vexed with him;
Who speaks most true is most dissembling;
He is my friend who has me crediting

D'ung cigne blanc que c'est ung corbeau noir;
Et qui me nuyst, croy qu'il m'ayde a povoir.
Bourde, verté, au jour d'uy m'est tout un.
Je retiens tout; rien ne sçay concepvoir,
Bien recueully, debouté de chascun.

Prince clement, or vous plaise sçavoir
Que j'entens moult et n'ay sens ne sçavoir;
Parcial suis, a toutes loys commun.
Que sais-je plus? Quoy? Les gaiges ravoir.
Bien recueully, debouté de chascun.

Ballade

Of each white swan that it's a raven here;
Who thinks to help me brings disaster near;
Jesting and truth, to me they are all one.
Remembering all, I yet see nothing clear—
Welcomed by all, and he whom all men shun.

Kind prince, I pray you that it please you hear
That I know much, yet have no sense to spare,
Am partisan, yet all laws bear me down.
What then? Make me once more your pensioner—
Welcomed by all, and he whom all men shun.

LE TESTAMENT XLVII–LVI[7]

LA VIEILLE EN REGRETTANT LE TEMPS DE SA JEUNESSE

ADVIS m'est que j'oy regreter
La belle qui fut hëaulmiere,
Soy jeune fille soushaitter
Et parler en telle maniere:
'Ha! vieillesse felonne et fiere,
Pourquoi m'as si tost abatue?
Qui me tient, qui, que ne me fiere,
Et qu'a ce coup je ne me tue?

'Tollu m'as la haulte franchise
Que beaulté m'avoit ordonné
Sur clers, marchans et gens d'Eglise:
Car lors il n'estoit homme né
Qui tout le sien ne m'eust donné,
Quoy qu'il en fust des repentailles,
Mais que luy eusse habandonné
Ce que reffusent truandailles.

'A maint homme l'ay reffusé,
Qui n'estoit a moy grant sagesse,
Pour l'amour d'ung garson rusé,
Auquel j'en feiz grande largesse.

LAMENT OF THE OLD WOMAN
REMEMBERING HER YOUTH

I HEAR the former beauty, she
Who used to be the *heaulmière*, sigh
For her lost youth, regretfully
Speaking thus of days gone by:
'Proud, pitiless old age, oh why
Should you have brought me down so soon;
And what's to stop me violently
Taking my life now, to be done?

'You have deprived me of the power
My beauty gave me over men;
Merchants, and churchmen, men of law,
For no man born but would have given
His every penny to me then,
However repentance changed his views,
Provided only he could gain
What even beggars now refuse;

'What to so many I did deny—
It wasn't very wise of me!—
And all for one ungrateful, sly
Boy that I loved too generously;

A qui que je feisse finesse,
Par m'ame, je l'amoye bien!
Or ne me faisoit que rudesse,
Et ne m'amoit que pour le mien.

'Si ne me sceut tant detrayner,
Fouler aux piez, que ne l'aymasse,
Et m'eust il fait les rains trayner,
S'il m'eust dit que je le baisasse,
Que tous mes maulx je n'oubliasse.
Le glouton, de mal entechié,
M'embrassoit . . . J'en suis bien plus grasse!
Que m'en reste il? Honte et pechié.

'Or est il mort, passé trente ans,
Et je remains vielle, chenue.
Quant je pense, lasse! au bon temps,
Quelle fus, quelle devenue!
Quant me regarde toute nue,
Et je me voy si tres changiee
Povre, seiche, megre, menue,
Je suis presque toute enragiee.

'Qu'est devenu ce front poly,
Cheveulx blons, ces sourcils voultiz
Grant entroeil, ce regart joly,
Dont prenoie les plus soubtilz;

Lament of the Old Woman Remembering Her Youth

Whoever else I cheated, he
Was never one; I gave him love
And he returned me cruelty,
Loved me for what I had to give.

'However much he bullied me
And wore me down, I loved him so
That though he dragged me brutally
Round by the hair, a kiss or two
Would make me quite forget my woe;
And then that crooked scoundrel came
And took me in his arms—and now
What have I gained but sin and shame?

'Well, he's been dead for thirty years
And I, grown old and grey-haired too,
Remember those good days with tears,
What once I was, what I am now:
And when I'm naked, then I know
How utterly changed I am by age,
Poor, skinny, shrivelled through and through—
I think of it, and shake with rage!

'Where's the smooth forehead I had once,
The arching eyebrows, the light hair,
The wide-set eyes whose pretty glance
Could take in even the connoisseur,

Ce beau nez droit grant ne petiz,
Ces petites joinctes oreilles,
Menton fourchu, cler vis traictiz,
Et ces belles levres vermeilles?

.   .   .   .   .   .

'Le front ridé, les cheveux gris,
Les sourcilz cheus, les yeux estains,
Qui faisoient regars et ris
Dont mains marchans furent attains;
Nez courbes de beaulté loingtains,
Oreilles pendantes, moussues,
Le vis pally, mort et destains,
Menton froncé, levres peaussues:

.   .   .   .   .   .

'Ainsi le bon temps regretons
Entre nous, povres vielles sotes
Assises bas, a crouppetons,
Tout en ung tas comme pelotes,
A petit feu de chenevotes
Tost allumees, tost estaintes;
Et jadis fusmes si mignotes! . . .
Ainsi en prent a mains et maintes.'

Lament of the Old Woman Remembering Her Youth

The dimpled chin, the small neat ear,
And straight nose, neither large nor small,
The beautiful red mouth, the clear
Good-looking face—where are they all?

'Forehead lined, and hair gone grey,
Hairless eyebrows, eyes quite dull,
That were smiling once and gay,
The cause of many a merchant's fall;
Hooked nose, far from beautiful,
Hairy ears with folds of skin,
Face all lifeless now and pale,
Flabby lips, nut-cracker chin.

'Lamenting thus the days gone by,
We sit together, poor foolish hags
On skinny haunches, wretchedly
Huddled like bundles of old rags
Around a fire of hempen tags,
Soon kindled and soon burnt away,
So dainty once, and now such hags!
But many and many end this way!'

LE TESTAMENT CLXXVIII

EPITAPHE

CY gist et dort en ce sollier,
Qu'amours occist de son raillon,
Ung povre petit escollier,
Qui fut nommé Françoys Villon.
Oncques de terre n'eut sillon.
Il donna tout, chascun le scet:
Tables, tresteaulx, pain, corbeillon.
Gallans, dictes en ce verset:

VERSET (OU RONDEAU)

Repos eternel donne a cil,
Sire, et clarté perpetuelle,
Qui vaillant plat ni escuelle
N'eut oncques, n'ung brain de percil.
Il fut rez, chief, barbe et sourcil,
Comme ung navet qu'on ret ou pelle.
Repos eternel donne a cil.

Rigueur le transmit en exil
Et luy frappa au cul la pelle,
Non obstant qu'il dit: 'J'en appelle!'
Qui n'est pas terme trop subtil.
Repos eternel donne a cil.

EPITAPH

Here lies, in this small chamber,
One that love's arbalest brought down,
A very poor and humble scholar
By the name of François Villon known,
Who never a yard of land did own
Yet gave you all he had, remember,
Basket, and board, and bread thereon;
Over him then let his friends murmur:

RONDEL

Grant, O Lord, eternal rest
And lasting glory to this soul
Who never was, with dish or bowl,
Or even a sprig of parsley blessed
But bald as a scraped turnip, dressed
For cooking—eyebrows, head, and jowl:
Grant rest!

Harsh justice exiled him, addressed
His backside with a spade, poor soul;
Although he called out; 'I appeal!' —
Not an ambiguous request!
Grant rest!

OLIVIER BASSELIN
& JEAN LE HOUX

OLIVIER BASSELIN (*fifteenth century*). *A Norman poet of whom little is known for certain, but who seems to have done no more than inspire, at the distance of more than a century, the poems by which he has been chiefly remembered. The legend we have of him is, however, solid and circumstantial. According to this we are indebted to him for the many songs of wine, cider, love, and war that bear his name, and also for the word 'vaudeville'. He was born at Vire, where he owned a mill beside the bridge of Vaux, so that the songs he wrote came to be known as the 'vau de vire', from which the modern word has come. He is said to have suffered both as a result of his good living and of the English invasions in the Hundred Years War, and to have died fighting against the English—though the word* Engloys *in the popular ballad about him could mean 'moneylenders'!*

'Alas! good Oliver Basselin,
Are we to hear no more of you?
Have the *English* put an end to you? . . .'[8]

So much for the legend. The presence, in the verses attributed to Basselin, of many marks of later origin, was accounted for by their having been edited, in 1610, by the Virois lawyer JEAN LE HOUX (*c. 1550–1616*); *but it now appears that Jean Le Houx was not editor but author (or all but author) of the best known of these verses,* including the two poems printed here. *It is known that he made a journey to Rome to get absolution from the sin of merely editing them, so it is not surprising if he did not admit to full authorship! Those 'vau de vire' which definitely date back to Basselin's time are naïve and often patriotic. Perhaps the real Basselin did not prefer his glass to his warlike helmet, and 'Engloys' meant 'English' after all!*

LA GUERRE ET LE VIN

HARDY comme un Cesar, je suis à ceste guerre
Où l'on combat armé d'un grand pot et d'un verre.
Plus tost un coup de vin me perce et m'entre au corps,
Qu'un boulet qui cruel rend les gens si tost morts.

Le cliquetis que j'ayme est celuy des bouteilles.
Les pipes, les bereaux, pleins de liqueurs vermeilles,
Ce sont mes gros canons qui battent sans faillir
La soif, qui est le fort que je veux assaillir.

Je trouve, quant à moy, que les gens sont bien bestes
Qui ne se font plus tost au vin rompre les testes,
Qu'aux coups de coutelas en cherchant du renom:
Que leur chaut, estant morts, si l'on en parle ou non?

De trop boire frappée, une teste en reschappe;
Sent bien un peu de mal, lorsque le vent la happe,
Mais, quand on a dormy, le mal s'en va soudain.
A ces grands coups de Mars, tout remede y est vain.

Il vaut bien mieux cacher son nez dans un grand verre:
Il est mieux asseuré qu'en un casque de guerre:
Pour cornette ou guidon, suivre plus tost on doit
Les branches d'hiere ou d'if, qui monstrent où l'on boit.

WAR AND WINE

I AM as brave as Caesar in this war
Armed to the very teeth with jug and glass;
Better a charge of wine that leaves no scar
Than bullets spilling life that soon must pass.

Give me the bottle's for the battle's clash,
Barrels and casks of rich vermilion wine
For my artillery with which to smash
This thirst that I invest and undermine.

As far as I can see the man's a clown
Who would not rather get his broken head
By drinking than by fighting for renown;
What use will his renown be when he's dead?

The head brought down by drinking can recover;
When the wind buffets it you feel some pain,
Then after a short sleep the trouble's over;
On battlefields all remedy is vain.

Better to hide your nose in a tall glass
Than in a casque of war, more safe, I think,
Than following horn and ensign, just to pass
Beneath the yew and ivy to a drink.

71

Olivier Basselin

Il vaut mieux, près beau feu, boire la muscadelle,
Qu'aller sur un rempart faire la sentinelle.
J'aime mieux n'estre point en taverne en defaut
Que suivre un capitaine à la bresche, à l'assaut.

Neanmoins, tout excez je n'aime et ne procure;
Je suis beuveur de nom et non pas de nature.
Bon vin, qui nous fais rire et hanter nos amis,
Je ne tiendray tousjours ce que je t'ay promis.

War and Wine

Better beside the fire drinking muscatel,
Here inside the tavern and never in default,
Than outside on the ramparts playing the sentinel
Or following a captain to the breach, to the assault!

But I dislike and do not seek excess.
Good drinker, not born drunkard, is my due.
Good wine, that makes for laughter and friendliness,
I've promised more than I can keep to you.

A SON NEZ

BEAU nez, dont les rubis ont cousté mainte pipe
    De vin blanc et clairet,
Et duquel la couleur richement participe
    Du rouge et violet;

Gros nez! Qui te regarde à travers un grand verre
    Te juge encor plus beau.
Tu ne ressembles point au nez de quelque here
    Qui ne boit que de l'eau.

Un coq d'Inde, sa gorge à toy semblable porte:
    Combien de riches gens
N'ont pas si riche nez! Pour te peindre en la sorte
    Il faut beaucoup de temps.

Le verre est le pinceau, duquel on t'enlumine;
    Le vin est la couleur
Dont on t'a peint ainsi plus rouge qu'une guisgne,
    En beuvant du meilleur.

On dit qu'il nuit aux yeux; mais seront-ils les maistres?
    Le vin est guarison
De mes maux: j'aime mieux perdre les deux fenestres
    Que toute la maison.

TO HIS NOSE

BRAVE nose, whose rubies cost such casks of rare
White wine and claret,
Whose splendid colour has so rich a share
Of red and violet,

Huge nose! The man who sees you through a glass
Thinks you a snorter,
In no way like the nose of the poor ass
Whose drink is water.

More scarlet than a turkey cockerel's throat,
Rich men have prayed for
A nose as rich; a work of so great note
Long years have paid for,

Long years of painting with a brush of glass
And vintage wine,
Until not even cherries can surpass
This nose of mine.

They say wine harms the eyes, but who is master?
Wine is the cure
Of all my ills—though windows meet disaster
The house stands sure.

CLÉMENT MAROT

CLÉMENT MAROT (1495–1544). *Had connexions with the fifteenth as well as the sixteenth century, with the Reformation as well as the Renaissance. Editor of Villon and translator of the psalms, he was also one of the first translators of Ovid, Virgil, and Lucan. His interest in the Huguenot movement drove him as an exile first to Bordeaux, and thence successively to Béarn, Ferrara, Venice, and, after a return to France, to Geneva; here he displeased Calvin—a thing the rich sensuousness of a poem like the 'Vineyard Knife' would seem to make inevitable!—and was expelled, to die at Turin.*

CHANSON XXXII

CHANGEONS propos, c'est trop chanté d'amours:
Ce sont clamours, chantons de la serpette:
Tous vignerons ont à elle recours,
C'est leur secours pour tailler la vignette;
O serpilette, ô la serpillonnette,
La vignolette est par toy mise sus,
Dont les bons vins tous les ans sont yssus.

Le dieu Vulcain, forgeron des haults dieux,
Forgea aux cieulx la serpe bien taillante,
De fin acier trempé en bon vin vieulx,
Pour tailler mieulx et estre plus vaillante.
Bacchus la vante, et dit qu'elle est séante
Et convenante à Noé le bon hom
Pour en tailler la vigne en la saison.

Bacchus alors chappeau de treille avoit,
Et arrivoit pour benistre la vigne;
Avec flascons Silenus le suyvoit,
Lequel beuvoit aussi droict qu'une ligne;
Puis il trepigne, et se faict une bigne;
Comme une guigne estoit rouge son nez;
Beaucoup de gens de sa race sont nez.

SONG OF THE VINEYARD KNIFE

ENOUGH of love; let's leave for something new
All that to-do, and sing the vineyard knife;
No grower of vines but has recourse to you,
Makes use of you to prune his vines; O knife,
My vineyard knife, my little vineyard knife,
Renewing life, you make my good vines grow,
From which year after year the rich wines flow!

Vulcan, the high gods' blacksmith, did design
This shape divine, in heaven hammered out
The white-hot steel, and dipped it in old wine
To give the fine edge temper; and the shout
Bacchus gave out proclaimed beyond a doubt
That even devout old Noah could not find
A knife for pruning vines more to his mind.

With vine leaves crowned, young Bacchus brings his slim
Curved blade to trim and bless the fruitful vine;
With flagons old Silenus follows him,
And from each rim, in one unbroken line,
Pours down the wine, tries dancing, lies supine;
And for a sign his nose is cherry-red;
Of his great family many men are bred.

CHANSON XXV

UNE pastourelle gentile
Et un berger, en un verger,
L'autrehier en jouant à la bille
S'entredisoient, pour abreger:
    Roger
    Berger,
    Legere
    Bergere,
C'est trop à la bille joué:
Chantons Noé, Noé, Noé.

Te souvient il plus du Prophete
Qui nous dit cas de si hault faict,
Que d'une pucelle parfaicte
Naistroit un enfant tout parfaict?
    L'effect
    Est faict:
    La belle
    Pucelle
A un filz du ciel advoué:
Chantons Noé, Noé, Noé.

CAROL

A SHEPHERD and a shepherdess
In an orchard where they played
At ball one day, and, briefly, this
Is what one to the other said:
      Lithe
      Shepherd lad,
      Blithe
      Shepherd maid,
We've played enough at ball, they said,
Let's sing Noël, Noël, instead.

Remember what the prophet said
In telling of the great things done
In heaven, how the perfect maid
Would bring to birth the perfect son;
      The thing
      Is done,
      We sing
      The son
Of the perfect maid on heaven's throne;
Sing Noël, Noël, everyone.

MELLIN DE SAINT-GELAIS

MELLIN DE SAINT-GELAIS (c. 1490–1558). *Student of philosophy, mathematics, and astrology. Poet at the brilliant court of Francis I, he was made almoner to the Dauphin and subsequently librarian at Fontainebleau palace. His neat, witty rhyming made him acceptable to the court—until the appearance of Ronsard, after which his popularity waned. Perhaps some of the bitterness he felt at this is expressed in 'On a Detractor'.*

MALÉDICTIONS

CONTRE UN ENVIEUX[9]

JE prie à Dieu, qu'il vous doint povreté,
Hiver sans feu, vieillesse sans maison,
Grenier sans bled en l'arriere saison,
Cave sans vin tout le long de l'esté.

Je prie à Dieu qu'à bon droit et raison
N'ayez chez vous riens qui ne vous desplaise,
Tant que pour estre un peu mieux à vostre aise
Vous pourchassiez d'estre mis en prison.

.   .   .   .

Je prie à Dieu, le Roy de Paradis,
Que, mandiant, vostre pain alliez querre,
Seul, incognu, et en estrange terre,
Non entendus par signes ne par dits.

Je prie à Dieu que vous puissiez attendre,
Qu'on ouvre l'huis une nuict toute entiere,
Tout en pourpoint dessous une gouttiere,
Et que la belle à vous ne veuille entendre.

.   .   .   .

ON A DETRACTOR

I PRAY for poverty for you,
With fireless winter, roofless age,
No grain in store, no cellarage
Of cooling wine the summer through.

I pray to God, in equity
To see that all you have displease
So gravely that for greater ease
You'll search for prison sanctuary.

I pray to God, the King of Heaven,
That you may have to beg your bread
Exiled, alone, uncomforted
By any words or gestures even.

I pray that you may have to wait
Outside a door a whole night through,
While a slow gutter drips on you,
And she cares nothing for your state.

PIERRE DE RONSARD

PIERRE DE RONSARD (1524–85). *Born of a noble family, he grew up in court life, travelling as a page to Scotland, Flanders, Germany, and Piedmont. Returning to France at 19, he became deaf, and turned to a literary life. He met du Bellay in 1548, and formed with him, Baïf, Belleau, and others the group which became famous as the 'Pléiade'. He shared to the full the interest of his age in the Classics, and introduced classical forms, notably the ode, into French writing; attaining in his shorter odes and his sonnets a rich but subtle perfection that marked him out in his own time, as since, as one of the greatest of French poets. He and his friends, as Mr. Belloc has said, 'fixed the literary renaissance of France at its highest point'. His 'Sonnets for Hélène', again to quote the same writer, 'are (with du Bellay's) the evident original on which the author of Shakespeare's Sonnets modelled his work.'*

ODE[10]

VERSON ces roses pres ce vin,
Pres de ce vin verson ces roses,
Et boivon l'un à l'autre, à fin
Qu'au cœur nos tristesses encloses
Prennent en boivant quelque fin.

.   .   .   .   .

Est-il rien sans elle de beau ?
La Rose embellit toutes choses,
Venus de Roses a la peau,
Et l'Aurore a les doigts de Roses,
Et le front le Soleil nouveau.

Les Nymphes de Rose ont le sein,
Les coudes les flancs et les hanches:
Hébé de Roses a la main,
Et les Charites, tant soient blanches,
Ont le front de Roses tout plein.

.   .   .   .   .

Bacchus, espris de la beauté
Des Roses aux fueilles vermeilles,
Sans elles n'a jamais esté,
Quand en chemise sous les treilles
Il boit au plus chaud de l'Esté.

ROSES

SCATTER by this jar of wine
Roses, in the scent of roses
Pledge one to the other, sign
That all griefs the heart encloses
May be drowned in roseate wine.

The rose is beauty's origin,
Adorning all by which she lingers;
Venus has a rosebud skin
And the dawn has rosy fingers;
The young sun has a ruddy mien.

The nymphs, they say, have breasts like roses,
Elbows, and hips, and thighs of rose;
Hebe's hands are made of roses,
And the Graces bind their brows,
Pale though they are, with crowns of roses.

Over Bacchus this complete
Conquest have red roses made:
Without them he will not sit
In shirt-sleeves in the leafy shade
Drinking through the summer heat.

ODE

A REMI BELLEAU

T U es un trop sec biberon
Pour un tourneur d'Anacreon,
Belleau, et quoy! ceste Comete
Qui naguiere au ciel reluisoit,
Rien que la soif ne predisoit
Ou je suis un mauvais prophete.

Les plus chauds Astres etherez
Ramenent les jours alterez
En ce mois pour nous faire boire:
Boy donques: apres le trespas,
Ombre, tu ne boiras là bas
Que je ne sçay quelle onde noire.

Mais non, ne boy point, mon Belleau,
Si tu veux monter au tropeau
Des Muses, desur leur montagne:
Il vaut trop mieux estudier
Comme tu fais, que s'allier
De Bacchus et de sa compagne.

Quand avecques Bacchus on joint
Venus sans mesure, on n'a point
Saine du cerveau la partie.
Donc pour corriger son defaut,
Un vieil pedagogue il luy faut,
Un Silene qui le chastie:

TO REMI BELLEAU

To think, Belleau, that such a man
As you translates Anacreon—
You drink so little! Did you see
The comet which not long since burst
And lit the sky? It foretold thirst,
Or I'm no use at prophecy!

These hot stars that in heaven blaze
Usher in parched and thirsty days
In order to make all men drink;
So drink, for after death we go
With other shades to drink below
At God knows what dark river's brink!

But no! On second thoughts, Belleau,
If you have set your mind to go
With the nine Muses on their mountain,
Keep on avoiding, as you do,
Bacchus and his unseemly crew,
Staying instead by learning's fountain.

And those who set out to combine
Venus with the God of Wine,
Say goodbye to sober sense.
Bacchus needs a pedagogue
To correct his fault and flog
Him well, as did Silenus once;

Ou les pucelles dont il fut
Nourry, quand Jupin le receut
Tout vif de sa mere bruslée;
Ce furent les Nymphes des eaux:
'Car Bacchus gaste noz cerveaux,
Si la Nymphe n'y est meslée.'

To Remi Belleau

Or else the young girls who were there
To care for him, when Jupiter
From his burned mother took him up;
That these were Water-Nymphs is plain:
'For Bacchus damages the brain,
Unless the Nymph is in the cup.'

SONNET

COMME on voit sur la branche au mois de May la rose
En sa belle jeunesse, en sa premiere fleur
Rendre le ciel jaloux de sa vive couleur,
Quand l'Aube de ses pleurs au poinct du jour l'arrose:

La grace dans sa fueille, et l'amour se repose,
Embasmant les jardins et les arbres d'odeur:
Mais batue ou de pluye, ou d'excessive ardeur,
Languissante elle meurt fueille à fueille déclose.

Ainsi en ta premiere et jeune nouveauté,
Quand la terre et le ciel honoroient ta beauté,
La Parque t'a tuée, et cendre tu reposes.

Pour obseques reçoy mes larmes et mes pleurs,
Ce vase plein de laict, ce panier plein de fleurs,
Afin que vif et mort ton corps ne soit que roses.

SONNET

As on a branch, in May, we see the rose
In her most lovely youth, in her first flower
Making the red sky jealous at the hour
When washed in dews of dawn her colour glows;

Her petals grace and sleeping love enclose,
And freshest scents on tree and garden shower;
But, beaten down by rain or the sun's power,
Drooping and dead, they one by one unclose.

So you, in your first glowing youth, with duty
Paid by both earth and heaven to your beauty,
Fate has cut off; in ashes you repose.

Now at your funeral accept my tears,
This vase of milk, this basket full of flowers,
Whose body, dead or living, is a rose.

ODE

A CASSANDRE

MIGNONNE, allons voir si la rose
Qui ce matin avoit desclose
Sa robe de pourpre au Soleil,
A point perdu ceste vesprée
Les plis de sa robe pourprée
Et son teint au vostre pareil.

Las! voyez comme en peu d'espace,
Mignonne, elle a dessus la place
Las las ses beautez laissé cheoir!
O vrayment marastre Nature,
Puis qu'une telle fleur ne dure
Que du matin jusques au soir!

Donc, si vous me croyez, mignonne,
Tandis que vostre âge fleuronne
En sa plus verte nouveauté,
Cueillez, cueillez vostre jeunesse:
Comme à ceste fleur la vieillesse
Fera ternir vostre beauté.

TO CASSANDRA

My Love, let us see if the rose
That we watched this morning unclose
Her crimson dress to the sun,
Has not lost, now evening is here,
Those tight crimson folds, or that clear
Fresh colour, so near to your own.

   Alas! in how little a time
The petals of her lovely prime
Lie strewn on the ground in our sight;
How utterly harsh Nature is
To let such a flower as this
Last only from morning till night.

   Believe me, my Love! in this hour
Before the first exquisite flower
And green tender freshness has past,
Gather in, gather in your first youth;
For, as with this flower, in truth
Your beauty will wither at last.

SONNET

HA je voudroy richement jaunissant
En pluye d'or goute à goute descendre
Dans le giron de ma belle Cassandre,
Lors qu'en ses yeux le somne va glissant.

Puis je voudroy en toreau blanchissant
Me transformer pour finement la prendre,
Quand en Avril par l'herbe la plus tendre
Elle va fleur mille fleurs ravissant.

Ha je voudroy pour alleger ma peine,
Estre un Narcisse, et elle une fontaine,
Pour m'y plonger une nuict à sejour:

Et si voudroy que ceste nuict encore
Fust eternelle, et que jamais l'Aurore
D'un feu nouveau ne rallumast le jour.

(Texte de 1578.)

SONNET

O, I could wish, most richly yellowing
To drops of golden rain, from heaven to shower
Into Cassandra's lap about the hour
When clouds of sleep her eyes are shadowing;

Or, made a bull by some such lavishing
Of dazzling whiteness, take and carry her
Gently through April fields, where like a flower
She walks, a thousand flowers ravishing;

And I could wish, my burning pain to cool,
I were Narcissus, she my fountain pool,
That in her waters I might plunge, and stay

The whole night through—and I could wish night drawn
Out to eternity, so that no dawn
Might ever light me to a coming day.

EPITAPHE DE FRANÇOIS RABELAIS

Si d'un mort qui pourri repose
Nature engendre quelque chose,
Et si la generation
Est faite de corruption:
Une vigne prendra naissance
De l'estomac et de la pance
Du bon Rabelais qui boivoit
Toujours ce pendant qu'il vivoit.
Car d'un seul trait sa grande gueule
Eust plus beu de vin toute seule
(L'epuisant du nez en deux cous)
Qu'un porc ne hume de lait dous,
Qu'Iris de fleuves, ne qu'encore
De vagues le rivage more.

Jamais le Soleil ne l'a veu
Tant fust il matin, qu'il n'eust beu,
Et jamais au soir la nuit noire,
Tant fust tard, ne l'a veu sans boire.
Car alteré, sans nul sejour
Le gallant boivoit nuit et jour.

Mais quand l'ardente Canicule
Ramenoit la saison qui brule,
Demi nus se troussoit les bras,
Et se couchoit tout plat à bas
Sur la jonchée entre les tasses,
Et parmy des escuelles grasses
Sans nulle honte se touillant
Alloit dans le vin barbouillant

EPITAPH ON RABELAIS

IF it's true that Nature can
Raise new life from a dead man,
And if generation
Springs out of corruption,
Then a vine should issue forth
From the stomach and huge girth
Of our Rabelais who contrived
To keep on drinking while he lived,
Who, with his mighty throat sucked down
Far more wine, all on his own,
Through nose and mouth, in a gulp or two
Than a porker drinking milk can do,
Than Iris from the rivers, or
From the waves of the African shore.

Nobody in morning sun
Ever saw him sober; none
From sunset until late at night
Saw him anything but tight;
Without pause our Rabelais
Kept on drinking night and day.

When the fiery dog-days brought
Round the season of the drought,
Half-dressed, with his sleeves rolled up,
He'd lie down flat beside his cup
Among the glasses on the rushes
Among the richly-loaded dishes,
Sprawling there quite shamelessly
Floundering as messily

Comme vue grenouille en la fange:
Puis yvre chantoit la louange
De son amy le bon Bacchus,
Comme sous luy furent vaincus
Les Thebains, et comme sa mere
Trop chaudement receut son pere,
Qui en lieu de faire cela
Las! tout vive la brula.

Il chantoit la grande massuë,
Et la jument de Gargantuë,
Le grand Panurge, et le païs
Des Papimanes ébaïs:
Leurs loix, leurs façons et demeures,
Et frere Jean des Antoumeures,
Et d'Episteme les combas:
Mais la mort qui ne boivoit pas
Tira le beuveur de ce monde,
Et ores le fait boire en l'onde
Qui fuit trouble dans le giron
Du large fleuve d'Acheron.

Or toy quiconque sois qui passes
Sur sa fosse répen des taces,
Répen du bril, et des flacons,
Des cervelas, et des jambons:
Car si encore dessous la lame
Quelque sentiment a son ame,
Il les aime mieux que les lis,
Tant soient ils fraichement cueillis.

As a frog does in the mud;
Then, when drunk, he'd sing aloud
The praises of his good friend Bacchus,
How he came to be victorious
Over the Thebans, how his mother
With such warmth received his father,
That, instead of making love,
He just burned her up alive!

Sing of Gargantua and his mare
And the huge staff he used to bear;
Splendid Panurge; and the domains
Of those gaping Papimanes,
Their houses, customs, and strange laws;
Of Friar John of Antoumeures;
And of the battles of Epistème;
But Death, who never drinks, took him,
The drinker, to the world below,
Where no other waters flow
Than the turbid streams that run
Down into wide Acheron.

Whoever happens to pass this way
Empty here a glass, I pray;
Pour out flagons, scatter cheese,
Legs of ham and sausages;
For if any feeling now
Animates that soul below,
These to lilies would be preferred
However freshly they were gathered!

ODE

A LA FONTAINE BELLERIE

O Fontaine Bellerie,
Belle fontaine cherie
De nos Nymphes quand ton eau
Les cache au creux de ta source
Fuyantes le Satyreau,
Qui les pourchasse à la course
Jusqu'au bord de ton ruisseau:

Tu es la Nymphe eternelle
De ma terre paternelle:
Pource en ce pré verdelet
Voy ton Poëte qui t'orne
D'un petit chevreau de lait,
A qui l'une et l'autre corne
Sortent du front nouvelet.

L'Esté je dors ou repose
Sus ton herbe, où je compose,
Caché sous tes saules vers,
Je ne sçay quoy, qui ta gloire
Envoira par l'univers,
Commandant à la Memoire
Que tu vives par mes vers.

L'ardeur de la Canicule
Ton verd rivage ne brule,

TO A FOUNTAIN

O LOVELY Bellerie,
Fountain as dear to me
As to the nymphs, your daughters,
Who run away to hide
In your cool depths from satyrs,
Chased to the very side
Of your protecting waters,

Still your eternal hands
Bless my paternal lands;
And I, your poet, this mead
And fresh green bank adorn
With a young suckling kid,
Each firstling of a horn
Just showing on his head.

In summer-time I doze
On your green banks, compose
On willow-shaded grass
These lines to send your fame
Out through the universe,
So that your gentle name
May live on in my verse

The heat of the dog-star
May not burn up your shore;

Tellement qu'en toutes pars
Ton ombre est espaisse et druë
Aux pasteurs venans des parcs,
Aux boeufs las de la charruë,
Et au bestial espars.

Iô, tu seras sans cesse
Des fontaines la princesse,
Moy celebrant le conduit
Du rocher percé, qui darde
Avec un enroué bruit
L'eau de ta source jazarde
Qui trepillante se suit.

To a Fountain

Always your region yields
Close shade beneath the boughs
To shepherds from the folds,
Tired oxen from the ploughs,
And cattle from the fields.

For ever the princess
Of fountains, I address
Your hoarsely-murmuring
Rock-conduit as it jets
Endlessly-following
Water that foams and frets
Babbling and chattering.

JOACHIM DU BELLAY

JOACHIM DU BELLAY (1525–60). *Lieutenant of the 'Pléiade', and author of its formal manifesto, 'Deffense et Illustration de la langue françoyse'. Like Ronsard, of noble birth, he accompanied his cousin, Cardinal du Bellay, on a diplomatic mission to Rome, and on his return was made a canon of Notre-Dame by a du Bellay who was Bishop of Paris. His sonnets show very clearly the effect of the decayed splendour of Roman civilization on a man of his time; and the most delicate of his shorter poems, 'A Winnower of Wheat to the Winds', is a translation from the Latin of Navagero. His 'Epitaphs' on his pet dog and pet cat suggest a whimsical tenderness; despite their slightness, it seems worth while printing these two poems in full for the informal details they give of the life of a nobleman of studious habits in a formal age. He was of a melancholy temperament, being sickly from childhood and dying at the early age of 35.*

EPITAPHE D'UN PETIT CHIEN

DESSOUS ceste motte verte
De lis et roses couverte
Gist le petit Peloton
De qui le poil foleton
Frisoit d'une toyson blanche
Le doz, le ventre et la hanche.
    Son nez camard, ses gros yeux
Qui n'estoient point chassieux,
Sa longue oreille velue
D'une soyë crespelue,
Sa queuë au petit floquet,
Semblant un petit bouquet,
Sa gembe gresle, et sa patte
Plus mignarde qu'une chatte
Avec ses petits chattons,
Ses quatre petits tetons,
Ses dentelettes d'ivoyre,
Et la barbelette noyre
De son musequin friand,
Bref tout son maintien riand
Des pieds jusques à la teste,
Digne d'une telle beste,
Meritoient qu'un chien si beau
Eust un plus riche tumbeau.
    Son exercice ordinaire
Estoit de japper et braire,

EPITAPH ON A PET DOG

BENEATH this turfy mound
With rose and lily crowned,
Lies little Peloton
Whose silky coat once shone
So white, fleece-like, and curly
On side, and back, and belly.
  His snub-nose and large size
Perfectly clear eyes,
His long soft silky ears
Matted with crinkly hairs,
His tail that wagged a gay
Tassel like a bouquet,
His slender leg, his paw,
As light upon the floor
As a cat's among its kittens,
His dugs like four neat buttons,
His little ivory teeth,
The smart black beard beneath
The dainty muzzle; stance,
And absurd countenance,
In fact each single feature
Of this deserving creature
Earned him the pleasantest
Of graves in which to rest.
  He used to spend his day—
In the ordinary way—

Courir en hault et en bas,
Et faire cent mille esbas,
Tous estranges et farouches,
Et n'avoit guerre qu'aux mousches,
Qui luy faisoient maint torment:
Mais Peloton dextrement
Leur rendoit bien la pareille:
Car se couchant sur l'oreille,
Finement il aguignoit
Quand quelqu'une le poingnoit:
Lors d'une habile soupplesse
Happant la mouche traistresse,
La serroit bien fort dedans,
Faisant accorder ses dens
Au tintin de sa sonnette
Comme un clavier d'espinette.
   Peloton ne caressoit
Si non ceulx qu'il cognoissoit,
Et n'eust pas voulu repaistre
D'autre main que de son maistre:
Qu'il alloit tousjours suyvant,
Quelquefois marchoit devant,
Faisant ne sçay quelle feste
D'un gay branlement de teste.
   Peloton tousjours veilloit
Quand son maistre sommeilloit,
Et ne souilloit point sa couche
Du ventre ny de la bouche,
Car sans cesse il gratignoit
Quand ce desir le poingnoit:

Epitaph on a Pet Dog

Barking and growling, chase
Himself from place to place;
With fierce outlandish cries
Levy his war on flies;
These teased him cruelly,
But he, most dexterously,
Gave what he got, would lie
On one ear, patiently
Watching the traitor light,
Letting him start to bite,
Then, with a loose, quick snap
Hold him there in the trap,
Immured as close as death;
And all the while his teeth
Kept time with his small bell
Like a spinet manual.

He did not leap to greet
Strangers, and he would eat
From his master's hand alone,
Always stayed round about
His heels when they went out,
Except when he ran on,
Keeping some secret, gay
Head-tossing holiday.

Peloton always kept
Watch while his master slept;
And did not soil his bed
In any way; instead
Would fuss and scratch about
Till someone let him out;

Tant fut la petite beste
En toutes choses honneste.

   Le plus grand mal, ce dict-on,
Que feist nostre Peloton,
(Si mal appellé doit estre)
C'estoit d'esveiller son maistre,
Jappant quelquefois la nuict,
Quand il sentoit quelque bruit,
Ou bien le voyant escrire
Sauter, pour le faire rire,
Sur la table, et trepigner,
Follastrer, et gratigner,
Et faire tumber sa plume,
Comme il avoit de coustume.
Mais quoy? nature ne faict
En ce monde rien parfaict:
Et n'y a chose si belle,
Qui n'ait quelque vice en elle.

   Peloton ne mangeoit pas
De la chair à son repas:
Ses viandes plus prisees
C'estoient miettes brisees
Que celuy qui le paissoit
De ses doigts amollissoit:
Aussi sa bouche estoit pleine
Tousjours d'une doulce haleine.

   Mon-dieu, quel plaisir c'estoit
Quand Peloton se grattoit,
Faisant tinter sa sonnette
Avec sa teste folette!

Epitaph on a Pet Dog

He was, as may be seen,
Exemplarily clean.

    Even the worst crimes done
By little Peloton
Were neither here nor there;
But sometimes he would hear
Noises and bark at night,
Breaking his master's sleep;
Or, seeing him start to write,
With one fantastic leap
He'd land right on the table,
And wildly scratch and scrabble,
Knocking over his pen;
A few such crimes, but then
Has nature ever yet
Made anything perfect?
Beauty that has no small
Blemish in it at all?

    At meals he did not eat
Much in the way of meat,
But much preferred to wait
While many a dainty crumb
Softened by finger and thumb
Came from his master's plate;
And right up to his death
He always had sweet breath.

    What fun it was to watch
The little fellow scratch,
His silly head shaking
And making his bell ring;

Quel plaisir, quand Peloton
Cheminoit sur un baston,
Ou coifé d'un petit linge,
Assis comme un petit singe,
Se tenoit mignardelet
D'un maintien damoiselet!
   Ou sur les pieds de derriere
Portant la pique guerriere
Marchoit d'un front asseuré,
Avec un pas mesuré:
Ou couché dessus l'eschine,
Avec ne sçay quelle mine
Il contrefaisoit le mort!
Ou quand il couroit si fort,
Qu'il tournoit comme une boule,
Ou un peloton, qui roule!
   Bref, le petit Peloton
Sembloit un petit mouton:
Et ne feut onc creature
De si benigne nature.
   Las, mais ce doulx passetemps
Ne nous dura pas long temps;
Car la mort ayant envie
Sur l'ayse de nostre vie,
Envoya devers Pluton
Nostre petit Peloton,
Qui maintenant se pourmeine
Parmi ceste umbreuse plaine,
Dont nul ne revient vers nous.
Que mauldictes soyez-vous,

What fun when Peloton
Along a pole would run,
Or sit up in a white
Cloth cap, just like a monkey,
Holding himself upright
Like a squireling of the gentry!
  Oh, I can see him now,
On two legs, with firm brow
And shouldered pike, march by,
Stepping so soldierly;
Or, when upon his spine,
He'd lie, and with quaint mien,
Pretend that he was dead;
Or suddenly run, and bowl
Head over heels, and roll
Along, a ball indeed!
  In short, my Peloton
Was such a lamb, no one
Could find another creature
Of so benign a nature.
  But Death was envious
Of our brief happiness,
My joy was cruelly
Taken away from me,
Poor Peloton had to go
Away to old Pluto,
And roam the shadowy plain
Whence none returns again.
My curses on the dread
Sisters who spin the thread

Joachim du Bellay

Filandieres de la vie,
D'avoir ainsi par envie
Envoyé devers Pluton
Nostre petit Peloton:
Peloton qui estoit digne
D'estre au ciel un nouveau signe,
Temperant le Chien cruel
D'un primtemps perpetuel.

Epitaph on a Pet Dog

Of fate, thus enviously
To take my dog from me.
They sent him down below
To live with old Pluto
Though he deserved translation
To a new constellation,
The Dog-Star tempering
With his perpetual spring.

EPITAPHE D'UN CHAT

MAINTENANT le vivre me fasche:
Et à fin, Magny, que tu sçaiche
Pourquoy je suis tant esperdu,
Ce n'est pas pour avoir perdu
Mes anneaux, mon argent, ma bource;
Et pourquoy est-ce donques? pource
Que j'ay perdu depuis trois jours
Mon bien, mon plaisir, mes amours:
Et quoy? ô souvenance greve!
A peu que le cueur ne me creve
Quand j'en parle, ou quand j'en escris:
C'est Belaud mon petit chat gris,
Belaud, qui fut paraventure
Le plus bel œvre que nature
Feit onc en matiere de chats:
C'estoit Belaud la mort aux rats,
Belaud, dont la beauté fut telle,
Qu'elle est digne d'estre immortelle.

Donques Belaud premierement
Ne fut pas gris entierement,
Ny tel qu'en France on les void naistre,
Mais tel qu'à Rome on les void estre,
Couvert d'un poil gris argentin,
Ras et poly comme satin
Couché par ondes sur l'eschine,
Et blanc dessous comme une ermine.

EPITAPH ON A PET CAT

MY life seems dull and flat,
And, as you'll wonder what,
Magny, has made this so,
I want you first to know
It's not for rings or purse
But something so much worse:
Three days ago I lost
All that I value most,
My treasure, my delight;
I cannot speak, or write,
Or even think of what
Belaud, my small grey cat
Meant to me, tiny creature,
Masterpiece of nature
In the whole world of cats—
And certain death to rats!—
Whose beauty was worthy
Of immortality.

Belaud, first let me say,
Was not entirely grey
Like cats bred here at home,
But more like those in Rome,
His fur being silver-grey
And fine and smooth as satin,
While, lying back, he'd display
A white expanse of ermine.

Petit museau, petites dens,
Yeux qui n'estoient point trop ardens,
Mais desquelz la prunelle perse
Imitoit la couleur diverse
Qu'on void en cest arc pluvieux,
Qui se courbe au travers des cieux.

La teste à la taille pareille,
Le col grasset, courte l'oreille,
Et dessous un nez ebenin
Un petit mufle lyonnin,
Autour duquel estoit plantee
Une barbelette argentee
Armant d'un petit poil folet
Son musequin damoiselet.

Gembe gresle, petite patte
Plus qu'une moufle delicate,
Si non alors qu'il desguaynoit
Cela dont il egratignoit:
La gorge douillette et mignonne,
La queuë longue à la guenonne,
Mouchetee diversement
D'un naturel bigarrement:
Le flanc haussé, le ventre large,
Bien retroussé dessous sa charge,
Et le doz moyennement long,
Vray sourian, s'il en fut onq'.

Tel fut Belaud, la gente beste,
Qui des piedz jusques à la teste,

Epitaph on a Pet Cat

Small muzzle, tiny teeth;
Eyes of a tempered warmth,
Whose pupils of dark-green
Showed every colour seen
In the bow which splendidly
Arches the rainy sky.

Plump neck, short ears, height
To his head proportionate;
Beneath his ebony nostrils
His little leonine muzzle's
Prim beauty, which appeared
Fringed by the silvery beard
Which gave such waggish grace
To his young dandy's face.

His slender leg, small foot—
No lambswool scarf could be
More soft, except when he
Unsheathed and scratched with it!
His neat and downy throat,
Long monkey's tail, and coat
Diversely flecked and freckled
In natural motley speckled;
His flank and round stomach
Under control, his back
Of medium length—you see
A mouser, obviously!

This was Belaud, a gentle
Animal, whose title

De telle beauté fut pourveu,
Que son pareil on n'a point veu.
O quel malheur! ô quelle perte,
Qui ne peult estre recouverte!
O quel dueil mon ame en reçoit!
Vray'ment la mort, bien qu'elle soit
Plus fiere qu'un ours, l'inhumaine,
Si de voir elle eust pris la peine
Un tel chat, son cueur endurcy
En eust eu, ce croy-je, mercy:
Et maintenant ma triste vie
Ne hayroit de vivre l'envie.

Mais la cruelle n'avoit pas
Gousté les follastres esbas
De mon Belaud, ny la soupplesse
De sa gaillarde gentillesse:
Soit qu'il sautast, soit qu'il gratast,
Soit qu'il tournast, ou voltigeast
D'un tour de chat, ou soit encores
Qu'il prinst un rat, et or' et ores
Le relaschant pour quelque temps
S'en donnast mille passetemps.
Soit que d'une façon gaillarde,
Avec sa patte fretillarde,
Il se frottast le musequin,
Ou soit que ce petit coquin
Privé sautelast sur ma couche,
Ou soit qu'il ravist de ma bouche
La viande sans m'outrager,

Epitaph on a Pet Cat

To beauty was so sure
He'd no competitor!
A sad and bitter cross!
Irreparable loss!
It almost seems to me
That Death, though he must be
More ruthless than a bear,
Would if he'd known my rare
Belaud have felt his heart
Soften—and for my part
I would not wince and shrink
So from life's joys, I think.

But Death has never watched
Him as he jumped, or scratched,
Laughed at his nimble tricks,
His many wild frolics,
Admired the sprightly grace
With which he'd turn, or race,
Or, with one whirl of cat,
Tumble, or seize a rat
And play with it—and then
Would make me laugh again
By rubbing at his jaw
With such a frisky paw
And such a dashing manner!—
Or when the little monster
Leapt quietly on my bed,
Or when he took his bread
Or meat most daintily

Alors qu'il me voyoit manger,
Soit qu'il feist en diverses guises
Mille autres telles mignardises.

Mon‑dieu, quel passetemps c'estoit
Quand ce Belaud vire‑voltoit
Follastre autour d'une pelote!
Quel plaisir, quand sa teste sotte
Suyvant sa queuë en mille tours,
D'un rouet imitoit le cours!
Ou quand assis sur le derriere
Il s'en faisoit une jartiere,
Et monstrant l'estomac velu
De panne blanche crespelu,
Sembloit, tant sa trongne estoit bonne
Quelque docteur de la Sorbonne!
Ou quand alors qu'on l'animoit,
A coups de patte il escrimoit,
Et puis appaisoit sa cholere
Tout soudain qu'on luy faisoit chere.

Voyla, Magny, les passetemps
Ou Belaud employoit son temps.
N'est il pas bien à plaindre donques?
Au demeurant tu ne vis onques
Chat plus addroit, ny mieulx appris
A combattre rats et souris.

Belaud sçavoit mille manieres
De les surprendre en leurs tesnieres,

Straight from my lips—for he
Showed in such various ways
His quaint engaging traits!

What fun to watch him dance,
Scamper, and skate, and prance
After a ball of thread;
To see his silly head
Whirl like a spinning-wheel
After his velvet tail;
Or, when he made of it
A girdle, and would sit
Solemnly on the ground
Showing his fluffy round
Of paunch, seeming to be
Learned in theology,
The spit of some well-known
Doctor at the Sorbonne!
And how, when he was teased,
He used to fence with us—
Yet if we stopped to fuss
Was very soon appeased!

O Magny, now you see
How he diverted me,
You'll realize why I mourn—
And surely no cat born
Has ever had so nice
A style with rats and mice!

He would come unawares
Upon them in their lairs,

Et lors leur falloit bien trouver
Plus d'un pertuis, pour se sauver:
Car onques rat, tant fust il viste,
Ne se vit sauver à la fuyte
Devant Belaud. Au demeurant
Belaud n'estoit pas ignorant:
Il sçavoit bien, tant fut traictable,
Prendre la chair dessus la table,
J'entens, quand on luy presentoit,
Car autrement il vous gratoit,
Et avec la patte friande
De loing muguetoit la viande.

Belaud n'estoit point mal⁄plaisant,
Belaud n'estoit point mal⁄faisant,
Et ne feit onq' plus grand dommage
Que de manger un vieux frommage,
Une linotte, et un pinson,
Qui le faschoient de leur chanson.
Mais quoy, Magny? nous mesmes hommes
Parfaicts de tous poincts nous ne sommes.

Belaud n'estoit point de ces chats
Qui nuict et jour vont au pourchas,
N'ayant soucy que de leur panse:
Il ne faisoit si grand' despense,
Mais estoit sobre à son repas,
Et ne mangeoit que par compas.

Aussi n'estoit⁄ce sa nature
De faire partout son ordure,

And not one could escape
Unless he'd thought to scrape
A second hole—no rat
Ever outran that cat!
And let me add at once
My Belaud was no dunce,
But very teachable,
Knowing how to eat at table—
When offered food, that is:
That eager paw you'd see
Held out so flirtingly
Might scratch you otherwise!

Belaud was well-behaved
And in no way depraved;
His only ravages
Were on an ancient cheese,
A finch and a young linnet,
Whose trillings seemed to get
On Belaud's nerves—but then
How perfect are we men?

He wasn't the sort to be
Out everlastingly
After more food to eat,
But was content to wait
Until his meals, when he
Ate without gluttony.

And he would never spread
His traces far and wide

Comme un tas de chats, qui ne font
Que gaster tout par ou ilz vont:
Car Belaud, la gentile beste,
Si de quelque acte moins qu'honneste
Contrainct possible il eust esté,
Avoit bien ceste honnesteté
De cacher dessous de la cendre
Ce qu'il estoit contrainct de rendre.

Belaud me servoit de joüet,
Belaud ne filoit au roüet,
Grommelant une letanie
De longue et fascheuse harmonie,
Mais se plaignoit mignardement
D'un enfantin myaudement.

Belaud (que j'ayë souvenance)
Ne me feit onq' plus grand' offense
Que de me réveiller la nuict,
Quand il entr'oyoit quelque bruit
De rats qui rongeoient ma paillasse:
Car lors il leur donnoit la chasse,
Et si dextrement les happoit,
Que jamais un n'en eschappoit.

Mais, las, depuis que ceste fiere
Tua de sa dextre meurtriere
La seure garde de mon corps,
Plus en seureté je ne dors:
Et or', ô douleurs nompareilles!
Les rats me mangent les oreilles:

Epitaph on a Pet Cat

Like many cats, who do
Havoc wherever they go.
If Belaud, dear creature,
Fell short in any feature
Of sheer propriety,
He had the modesty
To cover under cinder
What he was forced to render.

He was my favourite plaything;
And not for ever purring
A long and tunelessly
Grumbling litany,
But kept in his complainings
To kitten-like miaowings.

My only memory
Of him annoying me
Is that, sometimes at night
When rats began to gnaw
And rustle in my straw
Mattress, he'd waken me
Seizing most dextrously
Upon them in their flight.

Now that the cruel right hand
Of death comes to demand
My body-guard from me,
My sweet security
Gives way to hideous fears:
Rats come and gnaw my ears,

Mesmes tous les vers que j'escris
Sont rongez de rats et souris.

Vray'ment les Dieux sont pitoyables
Aux pauvres humains miserables,
Tousjours leur annonçant leurs maulx,
Soit par la mort des animaulx,
Ou soit par quelque autre presage,
Des cieux le plus certain message.

Le jour que la sœur de Cloton
Ravit mon petit Peloton,
Je dis, j'en ay bien souvenance,
Que quelque maligne influence
Menassoit mon chef de la hault,
Et c'estoit la mort de Belaud:
Car quelle plus grande tempeste
Me pouvoit fouldroyer la teste?

Belaud estoit mon cher mignon,
Belaud estoit mon compagnon
A la chambre, au lict, à la table,
Belaud estoit plus accointable
Que n'est un petit chien friand,
Et de nuict n'alloit point criand
Comme ces gros marcoux terribles,
En long miaudemens horribles:
Aussi le petit mitouard
N'entra jamais en matouard:
Et en Belaud, quelle disgrace!
De Belaud s'est perdue la race.

Epitaph on a Pet Cat

And mice and rats at night
Chew up the lines I write!

The gods have sympathy
For poor humanity;
An animal's death foretells
Some evil that befalls,
For heaven can speak by these
And other presages.

The day fate cruelly
Took my small dog from me—
My Peloton—the sense
Of evil influence
Filled me with utter dread;
And then I lost my cat:
What crueller storm than that
Could break upon my head?

He was my very dear
Companion everywhere,
My room, my bed, my table,
Even more companionable
Than a little dog: for he
Was never one of those
Monsters that hideously
Fill night with their miaows;
And now he can't become,
Poor little puss, a tom—
Sad loss, by which his splendid
Line is abruptly ended.

Joachim du Bellay

Que pleust à Dieu, petit Belon,
Que j'eusse l'esprit assez bon,
De pouvoir en quelque beau style
Blasonner ta grace gentile,
D'un vers aussi mignard que toy:
Belaud, je te promets ma foy,
Que tu vivrois, tant que sur terre
Les chats aux rats feront la guerre.

Epitaph on a Pet Cat

God grant to me, Belaud,
Command of speech to show
Your gentle nature forth
In words of fitting worth,
Your qualities to state
In verse as delicate,
That you may live while cats
Wage mortal war on rats.

SONNET

NOUVEAU venu, qui cherches Rome en Rome
Et rien de Rome en Rome n'apperçois,
Ces vieux palais, ces vieux arcz que tu vois,
Et ces vieux murs, c'est ce que Rome on nomme:

Voy quel orgueil, quelle ruine: et comme
Celle qui mist le monde sous ses loix,
Pour donter tout, se donta quelquefois,
Et devint proye au temps, qui tout consomme.

Rome de Rome est le seul monument,
Et Rome Rome a vaincu seulement.
Le Tibre seul, qui vers la mer s'enfuit,

Reste de Rome. O mondaine inconstance!
Ce qui est ferme, est par le temps destruit,
Et ce qui fuit, au temps fait resistance.

SONNET

NEWCOMER, you who look in Rome for Rome
And not a sign of Rome in Rome can see,
These palaces, this ruined masonry
Of wall and arch still bear the name of Rome:

But what huge pride and what a fall! Her fame,
Her laws once held the world in sovereignty;
Seeking to conquer all, she bent the knee,
And now time has consumed all but her name.

This Rome is but Rome's monument and tomb,
All-conquering Rome has only conquered Rome.
The Tiber, ever-moving towards the sea,

Is all that stands of Rome—O fickle world,
Where firm, enduring things to ruin are hurled
And passing things resist eternally!

SONNET

QUI voudra voir tout ce qu'ont peu nature,
L'art et le ciel (Rome) te vienne voir:
J'entens s'il peult ta grandeur concevoir
Par ce qui n'est que ta morte peinture.

Rome n'est plus: et si l'architecture
Quelque umbre encor de Rome fait revoir,
C'est comme un corps par magique sçavoir
Tiré de nuict hors de sa sepulture.

Le corps de Rome en cendre est devallé,
Et son esprit rejoindre s'est allé
Au grand esprit de ceste masse ronde.

Mais ses escripts, qui son loz le plus beau
Malgré le temps arrachent du tumbeau,
Font son idole errer parmy le monde.

SONNET

HE who would like to see what art and nature
And heaven can achieve should visit Rome,
That is, if he knows how to guess the sum
Of greatness from his glimpse of a dead picture.

Rome is no more; and if her architecture
Can throw before us shadows of old Rome
It is as if some corpse should leave his tomb
And walk at night by a magician's order.

The bones of Rome in dust and ashes fall;
The soul of Rome has gone to make its home
With the great spirit of this earthly ball;

But her great writings, snatching from the tomb,
Despite of time, the praise of her past worth,
Have sent her image wandering through the earth.

SONNET

JE hay du Florentin l'usuriere avarice,
Je hay du fol Sienois le sens mal arresté,
Je hay du Genevois la rare verité,
Et du Venetien la trop caute malice:

Je hay le Ferrarois pour je ne sçay quel vice,
Je hay tous les Lombards pour l'infidelité,
Le fier Napolitain pour sa grand' vanité,
Et le poltron Romain pour son peu d'exercice:

Je hay l'Anglois mutin et le brave Escossois,
Le traistre Bourguignon et l'indiscret François,
Le superbe Espaignol et l'yvrongne Thudesque:

Bref, je hay quelque vice en chasque nation,
Je hay moymesme encor' mon imperfection,
Mais je hay par sur tout un sçavoir pedantesque.

SONNET

I HATE the money-lending avarice
Of Florentines, the violent Siennese,
The very rarely truthful Genoese,
The sly Venetian's subtle artifice,

The Neapolitan's vanity, some vice
That I've forgotten in the Ferrarese;
I hate all Lombards and their treacheries,
The cowardly Roman's unpreparedness;

I hate the surly Englishman, swaggering Scot,
The talkative Frenchman, false Burgundian,
The arrogant Spaniard and the German sot;

I hate some vice or other in every nation,
And in myself a hundred vices find—
But none I hate like a pedantic mind.

SONNET

HEUREUX qui, comme Ulysse, a fait un beau voyage,
Ou comme cestuy là qui conquit la toison,
Et puis est retourné, plein d'usage et raison,
Vivre entre ses parents le reste de son aage!

Quand revoiray-je, helas, de mon petit village
Fumer la cheminee: et en quelle saison
Revoiray-je le clos de ma pauvre maison,
Qui m'est une province, et beaucoup d'avantage?

Plus me plaist le sejour qu'ont basty mes ayeux,
Que des palais Romains le front audacieux:
Plus que le marbre dur me plaist l'ardoise fine,

Plus mon Loyre Gaulois que le Tybre Latin,
Plus mon petit Lyré que le mont Palatin,
Et plus que l'air marin la doulceur Angevine.

SONNET

HAPPY as Ulysses, his voyage done,
Or he who went to get the Golden Fleece,
The traveller who returns to live in peace
In his own place, rich in experience grown!

When shall I see my village, and my own
Fireside with warm smoke rising, find my ease
Within my own small house, on lands that please
Me better than a province or a throne?

Better the walls of my ancestral home
Than the proud-fronted palaces of Rome,
Fine slate than all their glittering marble too;

For me, French Loire surpasses Tiber still,
Better my Lyré than the Palatine Hill,
Than ocean winds the soft air of Anjou.

D'UN VANNEUR DE BLÉ
AUX VENTS

A vous troppe legere,
Qui d'æle passagere
Par le monde volez,
Et d'un sifflant murmure
L'ombrageuse verdure
Doulcement esbranlez,

J'offre ces violettes,
Ces lis et ces fleurettes,
Et ces roses icy,
Ces vermeillettes roses,
Tout freschement écloses,
Et ces œilletz aussi.

De vostre doulce halaine
Eventez ceste plaine,
Eventez ce sejour:
Ce pendant que j'ahanne
A mon blé, que je vanne
A la chaleur du jour.

A WINNOWER OF WHEAT
TO THE WINDS

To you, light throng,
On aery wing,
Through the world blowing;
The shady verdure
To whispering murmur
Stirred by your going:

I offer roses,
Lilies, and posies
Of violets to you,
The little red roses
This moment uncloses,
And these new pinks too.

With your sweet breath blow
Across this plain now;
Fan cool, I pray,
This place where I sweat
As I winnow my wheat
In the heat of the day.

LOUISE LABÉ

LOUISE LABÉ (1526–66), 'La Belle Cordière' of Lyons, comes fittingly at the end of a period Christine de Pisan all but began. She has been called the greatest woman poet since Sappho, and indeed both her life and achievement incite to extravagance. Strikingly beautiful, an expert rider and fencer, she is said to have worn armour and fought as a man—le Capitaine Loys—at the siege of Perpignan. She was a leader, with Maurice Scève, of the Lyons school at a time when Italy, Germany, Switzerland, and France met at Lyons, and literature flourished on a basis of industrial wealth outside the limiting influence of the Sorbonne in Paris and the Inquisition in Toulouse. Her love-poems have a fire and subtlety that mark her out, with Ronsard and du Bellay, as belonging to the end of this formal era. In France, owing to Malherbe and the French Academy, the succeeding era was formal, too; it was in England that the first free flowering of Post-Renaissance poetry took place.

ELEGIE[II]

LE tems met fin aus hautes Pyramides,
Le tems met fin aus fonteines humides:
Il ne pardonne aus braves Colisées,
Il met à fin les viles plus prisées,
Finir aussi il ha acoutumé
Le feu d'Amour tant soit il allumé:
Mais, las! en moy il semble qu'il augmente
Avec le tems, et que plus me tourmente.
Paris ayma Œnone ardamment,
Mais son amour ne dura longuement,
Medée fut aymée de Jason,
Qui tot apres la mit hors sa maison.
Si meritoient elles estre estimées,
Et pour aymer leurs Amis, estre aymées.
S'estant aymé on peut Amour laisser,
N'est il raison, ne l'estant, se lasser?
N'est il raison te prier de permettre,
Amour, que puisse à mes tourmens fin mettre?
Ne permets point que de Mort face espreuve,
Et plus que toy pitoyable la treuve:
Mais si tu veus que j'ayme jusqu'au bout,
Fay que celui que j'estime mon tout,
Qui seul me peut faire plorer et rire,
Et pour lequel si souvent je soupire,
Sente en ses os, en son sang, en son ame
Ou plus ardente, ou bien egale flame.
Alors ton faix plus aisé me sera,
Quand avec moy quelcun le portera.

FROM 'ELEGY'

TIME makes an ending of the Pyramids,
Time dries up the fountains in their beds,
On splendid Coliseums has no pity,
And makes an ending of our dearest city;
It has a way of ending, in their turn,
Our fires of love, however well they burn;
But these in my case grow more violent
As time goes by, and cause me more torment.
Although the love of Paris was so strong,
Oenone did not keep it very long;
Medea, loved so short a while before,
Was turned away by Jason from his door.
These loved their loves so well they surely proved
That they deserved in their turn to be loved;
And if by those loved love is so neglected
Then those who are *not* loved might be expected
To tire of love, and you, love, should allow
The pains I suffer to be ended now.
Do not, I beg you, make me try to prove
That even death is kindlier than love;
And if you wish me to love steadfastly
See that the one who means the world to me,
With power to make me laugh and make me cry
And at all hours of the day to sigh,
Feels in his very soul, his blood, his bone,
A love at least the equal of my own.
I'd bear my burden far more easily
With someone else to share its weight with me.

SONNET

TOUT aussi tot que je commence à prendre
Dens le mol lit le repos desiré,
Mon triste esprit hors de moy retiré
S'en va vers toy incontinent se rendre.

Lors m'est avis que dedens mon sein tendre
Je tiens le bien, où j'ay tant aspiré,
Et pour lequel j'ay si haut souspiré,
Que de sanglots ay souvent cuidé fendre.

O dous sommeil, ô nuit à moy heureuse!
Plaisant repos, plein de tranquilité,
Continuez toutes les nuits mon songe:

Et si jamais ma povre ame amoureuse
Ne doit avoir de bien en verité,
Faites au moins qu'elle en ait en mensonge.

SONNET

As soon as I begin to overtake
On my soft bed the sleep I'm longing for,
I seem to feel my lonely soul withdraw
And without waiting for your presence make;

And then, at last, my aching arms can take
And hold, it seems, the joy I've waited for,
That I have sighed so long and deeply for,
And sobbed for till I thought my heart would break.

O gentle sleep, most happy, happy night,
Delightful rest, full of tranquillity,
May I, night after night, know this illusion;

And if for ever you withhold delight,
Never allow me the reality,
At least may I preserve this dear delusion.

MARIE STUART

MARIE STUART (1542–87). *The career and tragic death of* MARY QUEEN OF SCOTS *are too well known to require comment. These lines, said to have been written when she left behind the familiar, civilized life of her adopted France for the inhospitable kingdom of Scotland, have also been attributed to an eighteenth-century journalist, but there is no final reason to suppose that she could not have written them, as she is known to have been the author of the 'triste et doux chant' on the death of her husband, Francis II. She was Queen of France from 1559 to 1560, and was not yet 19 when she made the five-day voyage from Calais to Leith in August 1561.*

ADIEUX A LA FRANCE

*(Vers écrits en vue des côtes de France,
sur le vaisseau qui conduisait la Reine en Écosse)*

ADIEU, plaisant pays de France,
     O ma patrie,
     La plus chérie,
Qui as nourri ma jeune enfance;
Adieu, France! adieu, mes beaux jours!
La nef qui disjoint nos amours
N'a cy de moi que la moitié;
Une part te reste, elle est tienne.
Je la fie à ton amitié
Pour que de l'autre il te souvienne.

FAREWELL TO FRANCE

*(Lines attributed to Mary Stuart, and said to have been
written on board the ship which took her to Scotland)*

GOOD-BYE to pleasant France,
　　To my own land,
　　Beloved land,
My childhood's land, my France;
Good-bye to my best days!
The ship which parts our ways
Leaves half of me behind,
Half of my love to be
Your own, and call to mind
The half which comes with me.

NOTES

[1] P. xi Steele, *The English Poems of Charles of Orleans,* line 4193: *nyse as purse of an ay* = delicate as the skin of an egg.

[2] P. 7.　Semé les fleurs et planté le rosier,
Aux ignorans de la langue pandras,
Grant translateur, noble Geffroy Chaucier.

[3] P. 20.　The stanza before the envoy falls below the rest of the poem in dignity. It reads:
Priez, galans joyeux en compaignie,
Qui despendre desirez a largesse,
Guerre vous tient la bourse desgarnie;
Priez, amans, qui voulez en liesse
Servir amours, car guerre, par rudesse,
Vous destourbe de voz dames hanter,
Qui maintesfoiz fait leurs vouloirs tourner;
Et quant tenez le bout de la couroye,
Un estrangier si le vous vient oster:
Priez pour paix, le vray tresor de joye!

[4] P. 38.　Given as an example of the trivialities that often formed the theme of rondel sequences: a nocturnal exploit of one Stephen Le Gout had ended with his having his cloak torn from his shoulders, and being forced to jump from a window in order to escape.

[5] P. 46.　Known as the 'Ballade des Pendus' and also as the 'Epitaphe en forme de Ballade, que feit Villon pour luy et ses compagnons, s'attendant estre pendu avec eulx'.

[6] P. 56.　Known as the 'Ballade Villon' or 'B. du concours de Blois'. It appears in a collection of twelve on the same subject by poets at the court of Charles d'Orléans. Although a set piece, the subject suited the greatest and most disreputable poet of the group.

7 P. 60. Also known as 'Les Regrets de la belle Heaulmière'. The word 'heaulmière' is untranslatable. It refers perhaps to the helmet-making trade, hence often translated 'armouress'; perhaps to a distinctive headgear worn by prostitutes. A well-known courtesan called La Belle Heaulmière was at the height of her beauty in 1415. The catalogue is incomplete without stanzas LIII and LV. These read:

> Ces gentes espaulles menues,
> Ces bras longs et ces mains traictisses,
> Petiz tetins, hanches charnues,
> Eslevees, propres, faictisses
> A tenir amoureuses lisses;
> Ces larges rains, ce sadinet
> Assis sur grosses fermes cuisses,
> Dedens son petit jardinet?
>
> . . . . . .
>
> C'est d'umaine beaulté l'issue!
> Les bras cours et les mains contraites,
> Les espaulles toutes bossues;
> Mamelles, quoy? toutes retraites;
> Telles les hanches que les tetes;
> Du sadinet, fy! Quant des cuisses
> Cuisses ne sont plus, mais cuissetes
> Grivelees comme saulcisses.

8 P. 69.   Hellas! Olivier Bassellin,
> N'orrons nous poinct de vos nouvelles?
> Vous ont les *Engloys* mys à fin? . . .

9 P. 84.   Extract only, but rest of poem not easily accessible. Stanzas 3, 6, 7, 8, 9, 10, 11 add to the picture of the time:

> Je prie à Dieu, que vous rencontriez seize,
> Toutes les fois que vous livrerez dix,
> Et qu'il vous doint deux maistres estourdis,
> Et un valet qui ne jamais se taise.

Je prie à Dieu que pour honneur acquerre
Et meriter couronne de laurier,
Vous ne pensiez qu'à vous tenir gaurier,
Brave en la paix et couard en la guerre.

Je prie à Dieu que sans hoste ou fourrier
Vous poursuyviez en la Cour quelque affaire,
Et qu'il vous doint, pour diligence faire,
Le trot rompu d'ung cheval de courrier.

Je prie à Dieu, qui seul peut tout parfaire,
Qu'à vous se vienne ung marchant attacher,
Qui nuict et jour ne face que prescher
De vostre debte et de luy satisfaire.

Je prie à Dieu, pour mieux vous empescher,
De vous donner cinquante deux procès,
Forte partie, un Juge sans accès,
Foible advocat, fors à prendre et pescher.

Je prie à Dieu qu'il vous pregne un accès
De froide peur et longue jalousie
Qu'un autre n'ayt vostre femme choisie
Pour l'espouser après vostre decez.

Je prie à Dieu que l'on ayt fantasie
Qu'ayant les maux qu'ay ici recité,
Vous ayez mieux que n'avez merité,
Et qu'on vous fait faveur et courtoisie.

¹⁰ P. 88. Extracts only. Stanzas 2, 3, 4, 5, 6, 7, 8, 11 easily accessible in the *Oxford Book of French Verse* and elsewhere.

¹¹ P. 148. Extract only. Complete poem in the *Oxford Book of French Verse*.